LEARNING
TO
PREACH

Biblical Preaching
in the Local Church

Jeremy McQuoid & Stephen McQuoid

opal   Partnership
Churches networking for mission

British Library Cataloguing in Publication Data

A catalogue record for this book is available from the British Library

ISBN 978-1-9160130-0-1

Typeset and cover design by projectluz.com
Printed and bound in Great Britain
for Partnership (UK) Ltd and OPAL Trust
by Bell & Bain, Glasgow

Series Preface

This book forms part of a series being published jointly by OPAL Trust[1] and Partnership[2] with the collaboration of GLO Europe[3] and Tilsley College[4]. The titles which are part of this *Learning to ...* series so far are:

David Clarkson and Stephen McQuoid, *Learning to Lead: Next Generation*, OPAL Trust, 2013

Stephen McQuoid, *Learning to Share the Good News: Evangelism and the Local Church*, OPAL Trust & Partnership, 2019

Jeremy McQuoid & Stephen McQuoid, *Learning to Preach*, OPAL Trust & Partnership, 2020.

These titles are an example of collaboration between bodies which serve a large group of independent local churches which are found in the UK and in possibly as many as 150 or more countries across the world.

The purpose of the series is to provide material of help to church leaders, and others who are active in church life and work, in local churches which,

---

1 **OPAL [Overseas Publishing and Literature] Trust** provides literature for the Majority World. It provides affordable Bibles and other good Christian literature to missionaries and national workers alike, in many countries worldwide, and has permanent book depots in Zambia and the USA, as well as in the UK.

2 **Partnership** has existed for a number of decades specifically to encourage, strengthen, and support local independent evangelical churches which are committed to the biblical gospel and to team leadership and every member ministry. One way in which it does this is through publications (including the thrice-yearly *Partnership Perspectives*) aimed particularly to help church leaders and other volunteer workers. It is in close contact with some 350 churches in the UK.

3 **GLO Europe** is a Christian mission organization dedicated to bringing the good news of Jesus to a world that is lost. Its vision is to establish church planting teams throughout Europe and to support them and local churches through short-term mission trips. It is also committed to training and equipping Christians for mission and ministry so that they can share God and their faith effectively.

4 **Tilsley College** is the training arm of GLO Europe and is based at Motherwell in Scotland. It offers a range of one-, two-, and three-year accredited residential courses at very economical fee-rates (all including siginificant, on-the-job placement experience), part-time study through open access to the College's regular teaching, evening class study in local areas (Joshua Training), and online study.

\

because they are committed to team leadership and every-member ministry, have many unpaid church leaders and other volunteers who are vital to the life of their churches. Many of these church workers have had little time and opportunity for formal training for their responsibilities: they are keen students of Scripture, have active devotional lives, and often much experience in the Christian service which they undertake. But, for the most part, as has been said of the armies of the American Civil War, they have learned 'to march by marching and to shoot by shooting'. Such leaders and workers are essential to the life and work of the church, and it is evidently impossible, and in principle gravely limiting, for Christian ministry to be carried out exclusively by trained, paid workers. But, very often, volunteer workers are only too conscious that they could do better if they had some 'continuous professional development' (CPD) for their tasks. It is the purpose of this series to provide relevant and helpful material which can be used in this way. For some topics in the series, the material will simply be print; while for others there will be related audio-visual material supplementing the print and a related training course which is accessible online (as is the case with *Learning to Lead*—see https://glo-europe.org/tilsley/learningtolead.html for more details).

While the aim of this series is to help voluntary Christian workers, we have no doubt that those who have had the privilege of formal training for Christian work, can profit from the books in this series, if only by way of 'brush-up' and CPD for themselves!

The books in this series are not produced for profit by commercial entities, nor do writers and editors normally receive remuneration for their work. Any surpluses on sales will be used to finance further such publications and to subsidize the distribution of books in the Majority World, so that church leaders and others can benefit from them when otherwise they would not be able to do so.

Contents

Preface

This book contains everything you need to think about when you are starting out to preach. Preaching may be an activity which is entirely new to you or you may have listened to preaching throughout your life. In either case, this book demonstrates how much mental, physical and spiritual effort lies behind what may seem no more than someone standing up and talking on a Sunday morning.

Learning to Preach brings together the knowledge and experience of its two authors. Stephen McQuoid is General Director of GLO Europe and a former Principal of Tilsey College, Motherwell, Scotland where he taught on the subjects he writes about here, and Jeremy McQuoid is Teaching Pastor of Deeside Christian Fellowship in Aberdeen, Scotland where he preaches regularly to a large congregation. Together they have built up a fund of relevant knowledge over the years which they want to share with you to help you to take your first steps in this important activity.

Learning to Preach explains why you need knowledge about the biblical text and how to read it, how to make sense of its different genres; it shows you how to move from understanding the text to moulding that understanding into a sermon which enables the message of the passage to be understood by others so that they can strengthen their own Christian lives. *Learning to Preach* introduces readers to historical traditions in preaching as well as providing up to date advice on the use of media for preaching in today's world. Although the writers underline the responsibility which rests on preachers, their advice is always very readable and deeply encouraging.

CHAPTER 1

Building Foundations:
The centrality of scripture in the life of the church

Jeremy McQuoid

I recently attended a large Christian conference in South Wales. It was a gathering of pastors and church leaders from various backgrounds who were all evangelical. We enjoyed a time of praise together with lively musical backing. There were a couple of interesting interviews about church strategy and then came the preaching.

When the preacher rose to his feet, I noticed that the lights were dimmed, leaving only one light shining on the preacher. The speaker was a gifted communicator and brought a message full of lively illustrations and anecdotes. But we barely looked at a verse of Scripture.

There was no rustling of pages. No one read a Bible passage. And even if they had done, no one could have seen their Bibles because the lights were off. There was no expectation that the preacher would explain anything about the word of God to us. There were a few stories, plenty of laughs and a 'feel good' factor. But it struck me that the preacher himself was the main focus, not the Bible.

This scenario reflects what has been happening more and more in the West, and, I suspect, in other parts of the world. The Bible is being neglected. Preaching is being reduced from forty minutes of Bible teaching to ten minutes of storytelling only loosely tied to Bible themes. The focus of attention is less on the word of God and more on the charisma of the preacher. And if this trend continues, our generation will grow deaf to the voice of God. This is serious!

How have we got here?

I can understand, in some ways, why the Bible has been neglected in modern day preaching. After all, it is an ancient book, at least 2000 years away from us in its culture. Understanding Scripture is hard work. Serious preaching demands hours of study and prayer to produce a stirring message. And often the Bible seems irrelevant in a world of internet, i-phones, and other huge advances in technology.

If we are honest many Christians have a growing embarrassment about some of the more bizarre stories in scripture – talking snakes in the Garden of Eden; God's bloodthirsty desire to wipe out the Canaanites; strange, hairy prophets like Elijah calling down fire from heaven. Can we really tell a modern audience that Jesus walked on water? It's easy to believe that someone fell asleep when Paul was preaching, but it is harder to accept that Paul brought the man back to life so that he could get to the end of his sermon!

You can understand people, who are desperate to show how the Christian message makes sense in a twenty-first century setting, wanting to downplay some of the awkward details of the Bible to get the basic message across in relevant and engaging ways. But there is a huge danger in removing the Bible from preaching.

No Bible = no Christianity

The church did not create the Bible, the Bible created the church. It was Peter's sermon in Acts 2, following the death and resurrection of Christ, where he called his hearers to 'repent and be baptized,' (Acts 2: 38) that started the movement we call Christianity. We are told '3000 people were added to their number that day' and the church was born (Acts 2: 41). Christianity sparked into life following the resurrection of Christ, the public preaching of that resurrection and how it fulfilled Old Testament promises. The Bible created the church, not the other way round.

And if you study the book of Acts, the book that reflects more than any other the rise and development of the church, you will discover that it is built on summaries of nine sermons, preached mostly by Peter and Paul, calling people to repentance and faith in Jesus Christ. Each of these sermons seeks to bring the message of the Old Testament by showing how Jesus fulfilled the ancient text to people who knew very little about the Bible.

The church would not exist if it were not for this sacred revelation of God come down to us through the inspired 'apostles and prophets' (Eph. 2: 20). So to move away from the Bible is like a tree trying to move away from its roots. Death and dryness will result.

The great theologian John Calvin, during the days of the Reformation, said that a church could only be a church if it emphasized three things: firstly proper church discipline – rules for appropriate behaviour in the church; secondly, the pure use of the sacraments – baptism and communion; and thirdly, and most importantly, was what Calvin called 'the pure teaching of the word of God.'[1] A church is not a church unless it preaches the pure word of God. The very definition of a church, its distinguishing mark, is the public declaration of the scriptures. That means declaring what God has said through the prophets and apostles, not the latest ideas of a pastor. It means tackling the issues God wants to tackle, not the 'felt needs' of people.

The American pastor, John Piper, said that he once preached a sermon series on the glory of God from the book of Isaiah. His messages were all about the character of God, with very little application for people in the pews. But at the end of the series, a couple came up to him who had given birth to a son with major learning difficulties. They said they felt strengthened in their daily struggles by the vision of the glory of God that Piper had given them while preaching God's Word in Isaiah. What seemed irrelevant was a profound blessing to a couple who were facing the biggest challenge of their lives. God's Word is sufficient for every situation we face in life.

I am not suggesting that preachers should avoid applying the text to the lives of their hearers. We will discover in this book how vital good application is. But it is a reminder that the power of preaching resides in the words of God, re-speaking what God has spoken in the Bible. That often means dealing with subjects like God's holiness, judgement, salvation and the future new heavens

---

1 J. Calvin. *Institutes of the Christian Religion*, 4.1.5

and new earth — subjects that seem far removed from modern life; subjects that you won't hear very much about on radio, television or over the internet, and certainly not the kind of subjects that people want to hear. Yet they are subjects that the eternal God wants to imprint on our hearts.

A biblical preacher comes to his text under the conviction that the power resides in 'preaching the Word', re-declaring what God has said, whether it seems relevant, or up-to-date in our culture, and even whether people want to listen or not. If we are truly preaching the word of God, many will not want to listen. The Bible itself warns us of that. Paul said that those who declare the eternal Gospel are to some the 'aroma of Christ' (2 Cor. 2: 15) but to others the 'stench from a rotting corpse' (MSG 2 Cor. 2: 16). But that should not stop us preaching the message of the Bible, straight and true, like an arrow to the human heart. The Bible is the source of divine power.

The power of the Word

The opening chapter of the Bible makes this point. The universe was created through God's word. The repeated refrain in Genesis 1 is '…and God said' and when God speaks, dramatic things happen. Light appears, darkness is dispelled, creatures come to life, stars shine, oceans roar, and demons tremble.

Ezekiel 37 says the same thing. The prophet, in captivity in Babylon, feels like many pastors today — he looks at Israel and all he can see is a valley of dry bones, a series of corpses, dead to God and dead to his word. And God asks the bewildered prophet 'can these bones live?' (Ezek. 37: 3). The answer is not 'tell the people what they want to hear'. Prophets in Israel's history were killed because they did not tell even kings and priests what they wanted to hear, but bravely declared the uncomfortable messages of judgement God had given them.

God's answer to Ezekiel is the inspiration for every preacher, 'Prophesy to these bones and say to them, 'Dry bones, hear the word of the Lord! … I will put breath in you, and you will come to life …Then you will know that I am the Lord' (Ezek. 37: 4—6). The life-giving power in preaching comes as the Holy Spirit (the breath of God) takes the word of God, declared boldly by frail, sinful men and breathes new life into the hearts of those who are spiritually dead.

No human wisdom or words can bring the life of God to dead people. The apostle Peter is adamant that we are 'born again,' we receive the life of God in us, only and always 'through the living and enduring word of God… the word of the Lord endures forever. And this is the word that was preached to you' (1 Pet. 1: 23—25).

The former Senior Pastor of Moody Church in Chicago, Dr Erwin Lutzer, had a very unusual approach to the preaching course he taught his students. He took them to a local cemetery and asked them to preach to the gravestones:

> Mr Smith, I want to tell you that Christ has died for your sins, and that he has risen again from the dead to give you eternal life. God is calling you to believe in his Son. Mr Smith, do you hear the voice of God?

You can picture the bewildered looks on the students, as they preached to the dead. But it is a class they never forget!

What preachers are doing is declaring the living word of God to men and women who are spiritually dead, as lifeless and insensitive to a preacher's voice as a corpse. And the only thing that will waken a spiritually dead man is the electricity of the word of God, a bold declaration from the Creator of the universe.

Preaching is a command from the 'living and enduring word of God', carried by the Spirit of God, like a sharp sword, to awaken a spiritual corpse. When you see the challenge of preaching from that perspective, the mere words of a man, the passing thoughts of a pastor, the latest psychological technique from a pulpit, really will not do. Only the living word of God can awaken the human soul, shining shafts of light into an otherwise impenetrable heart. When you preach, make sure it is the Bible you are preaching and pray for the breath of God to quicken people's corrupt souls.

The danger of 'false teaching'

If we are teaching people something other than the pure word of God, we can lead them astray, into what Paul calls 'hollow and deceptive philosophy, which depends on human tradition and the elemental spiritual forces of this world rather than on Christ' (Col. 2: 8). Paul was worried not simply that the

Colossians were replacing God's Word with something trivial, but they were teaching and listening to dangerous human philosophies that took people away from Christ.

It is a danger that the New Testament warns us about. We should not move away, even subtly, from declaring the truth of scripture, and replace it with the latest theories, or human teaching that brings a smile to people's faces. We are not here to be people pleasers, but to preach the Word which is 'alive and active. Sharper than any double-edged sword, it penetrates even to dividing soul and spirit, joints and marrow; it judges the thoughts and attitudes of the heart' (Heb. 4: 12).

The message of Israel's prophets rarely left people feeling comfortable. You know when you have truly heard God's Word preached, because a spotlight has been placed on your soul. God's scalpel goes to work on your deepest motives, and he weeds out what doesn't belong. Biblical preaching 'afflicts the comfortable and comforts the afflicted'.

That is why we need to be wary of the 'prosperity teaching' that is so popular in the Majority World. It is very tempting to preach to poor people, that if you give your best to God, he will make you healthy, wealthy and fulfil all your dreams.

That is a lie! Half the New Testament was written from a prison cell, and eleven out of Jesus' twelve apostles were martyred for the message they preached, yet they were deeply faithful to God. Paul speaks about his persecutions, shipwrecks, stonings and the days he went without food. He delighted in his weaknesses so that God's glory could shine through him.

Those who preach a prosperity gospel of wealth, health and success have cut themselves adrift from the lifestyles of the apostles in scripture and the many Bible passages that speak of the necessity and value of suffering. Jesus said, 'whoever wants to save their life will lose it, but whoever loses their life for me and the gospel, will save it' (Mk. 8: 35).

Preach the Word

When the apostle Paul was reaching the end of his life, he sent an emotionally-charged letter from his prison cell to his young apprentice, Timothy. The letter of 2 Timothy is worth memorizing for every pastor and preacher. What was Paul most keen to pass on to Timothy, in his dying words, his 'last will and testament'?

The crescendo of the book begins at the end of chapter three:

> … continue in what you have learned and have become convinced of, because you know from whom you learned it, and how from infancy you have known the Holy Scriptures, which are able to make you wise for salvation through faith in Christ Jesus. All scripture is God-breathed and is useful for teaching, rebuking, correcting and training in righteousness, so that the servant of God may be thoroughly equipped for every good work. In the presence of God and of Christ Jesus, who will judge the living and the dead, and in view of his appearing and his kingdom, I give you this charge:
>
> Preach the word; be prepared in season and out of season; correct, rebuke and encourage—with great patience and careful instruction (2 Tim. 3.14—4.2).

The Scriptures are to be a preacher's food and drink. Scripture is 'God-breathed' (2 Tim. 3: 16). The idea here is that the Bible writers were like a sail boat which the Spirit of God was blowing in the direction he wanted. God's Word is authoritative and powerful, like no other words.

And you can almost hear a drum roll in the background as Paul gives his final, pointed command to Timothy. It is as if Paul said,

> 'If you forget everything else I have said Timothy, remember this. Preach the Word. Preach it in season and out of season, when people want to hear and especially when they don't. The days will come, Timothy, when people even in the church will be repelled by the truth of God's Word. They won't want to hear about sin and the cross of Christ and coming judgement. So instead they will select teachers who will make them laugh, make them cry, who 'tickle their itching ears', charismatic storytellers who will avoid the hard edges of God's truth and preach a message people want to hear. When that

happens, don't lose your focus. Keep preaching the Word. Keep opening and studying what the Scriptures teach and present God's message, unadulterated, unedited, straight and true, even if you have to suffer for it (and you will). In the presence of God and his holy angels, and Christ Jesus the judge of all the earth — who will hold us accountable for what we teach and inspire us when we devote ourselves to unpopular truth – preach the Word! (see 2 Tim. 4: 1-4)

Expository preaching

Before we finish this chapter, let me explain what biblical preaching looks like. It means preaching passage-by-passage, book-by-book through the Bible, making sure that the message you are bringing to people is the message contained in the text.

That means working hard at understanding, for example, what Paul is saying to Timothy, and the context in which he says it (more of that later in the book). If I am preaching Mark 1: 1-8, my job as a preacher is to study what Mark is saying, his progression of thought, and then to teach the people how Mark's message applies to their lives.

It does not mean choosing a phrase from Mark 1: 1-8 that interests me and using that phrase as a springboard to say what I want to say to the people, rather than what God wants to say. You can only be sure the word of God has been preached when you are 're-speaking what God has spoken' through Mark.

When you read Mark 1 you notice he quotes from the prophet Isaiah, so as a preacher I need to understand what Isaiah was saying, why he was saying it, how Mark is using that quotation and then, what it says about Jesus and the Gospel Mark is presenting.

It is hard work. But if you come to the text each time, praying for illumination from the Spirit who inspired the text, asking God to open the treasures of his Word to you, you will make discoveries that will change your own life and the lives of your hearers, and you will never want to go back to 'people-centred' sermons again.

CHAPTER 2

Using the Prophetic Voice:
The history of preaching

Jeremy McQuoid

I had lunch with a man in my church recently who had endured a very disappointing year. His oil company had sent him to an office in Paris to develop the French side of the business. He and his wife had prepared themselves psychologically and physically for the move. But within nine months, his company sent him back home again, causing great upheaval in the family, because they wanted to re-structure the business.

I asked him how he felt about his company following the chaos it had brought to his life. He was surprisingly upbeat and forgiving. The reason for his understanding demeanour was because he had studied the history of the company from its small beginnings thirty years earlier, ironically in France. His passion for the company meant he could filter whatever disappointments came his way because he was able to keep a 'big picture' of where the company had come from. He felt inspired by its growth and was willing to absorb personal disappointments because he felt himself part of this bigger story. (How his wife reacted is another story!)

Having a basic grasp of the history of preaching has that kind of impact. You start to feel the passions of those from the past who have climbed into pulpits with nervous expectation, or who have spoken to hostile crowds in the open air. Every modern-day preacher walks in the footsteps of great men and women who have experienced the highs and lows of preaching the Word.

What is most encouraging about the history of preaching is the legacy that faithful, biblical preachers have left behind — a legacy of millions coming to Christ; and churches strengthened in the midst of turmoil and persecution. Great preaching has influenced presidents and princes. Biblical preaching works. Don't lose sight of that if you are feeling discouraged at the moment. Every preacher gets discouraged but that should not stop them obeying Christ's call to preach the Word with power.

The theologian PT Forsyth said, 'with its preaching Christianity stands or falls'.[2] That is a dramatic statement, but when you study the history of Christian preaching, you realize the church was at its strongest when preaching was at its best. Similarly, the decline of the church can be traced back to the decline of bold preaching, and a loss of confidence in the Bible. History shows that biblical preaching matters and has more enduring power than any other form of human communication.

Old Testament 'Preaching'

Any proper survey of the history of preaching must begin with the Old Testament. The great prophets of Israel - Isaiah, Jeremiah, Ezekiel and others - received direct oracles from God which they proclaimed. They usually introduced these oracles by saying 'thus saith the Lord'. There was a real authority behind what they said. They did not invent their messages on a whim. It was their job to speak exactly what God told them to say.

One of the more comical episodes of the Old Testament involves the false prophet Balaam who was paid to preach curses against Israel, but instead, and against his own will, God turned his curses into blessing. What this false prophet said to King Balak is a key conviction that every preacher needs to take into the pulpit:

---

2 P.T. Forsyth, *Positive Preaching and the Modern Mind*, London: Hodder and Stoughton 1907, p. 1.

> …if Balak should give me all the silver and gold in his palace,
> I could not do anything of my own accord, good or bad, to
> go beyond the command of the Lord—and I must say only
> what the Lord says…(Num. 24: 13).

The pulpit is not a place to say what we want to say, but to declare God's eternal word to his people. While the prophets had great authority, it was a derived authority that came from faithfully delivering what God had given them. One of the great scenes of the Old Testament is when the wicked King Ahab of Israel wants prophetic direction about a battle.

All the (false) prophets in his court are telling him exactly what he wants to hear. But the prophet Micaiah has been sent to prison by the king because he 'never prophesies anything good about me, but always bad' (1 Kgs 22: 8). Clearly Micaiah was not out to be popular, but to communicate God's word faithfully, and he was willing to suffer for preaching judgement on a king.

Ahab wants to know whether he should go into battle, and all his false prophets are telling him 'O yes, King. Victory is assured' (see v.12). So Ahab seeks Micaiah's counsel. But to begin with, Micaiah says with great irony, 'sure King, go and fight and you will win' (see v.15).

Ahab realizes that Micaiah is being sarcastic, so he presses him further and Micaiah comes out with one of the most amazing statements in the Bible:

> 'I saw the Lord sitting on his throne…
> And the Lord said, "Who will entice Ahab into attacking
> Ramoth Gilead and going to his death there?"…
> [A] spirit came forward, stood before the Lord and said, "I
> will entice him."
> "By what means?" the Lord asked.
> "I will go out and be a deceiving spirit in the mouth of all
> his prophets," he said.
> "You will succeed in enticing him," the Lord said. "Go and
> do it."
> So now the Lord has put a deceiving spirit in the mouths of all
> these prophets of yours; the Lord has decreed disaster for you.'
> (1 Kgs 22: 19-23)

Several important themes for preachers emerge from this intriguing story. Preachers are called to be bold. Telling a king who could have you murdered that God was going to bring disaster on him was not a place of safety. True preachers will suffer for what they preach, as Micaiah, Jeremiah and Isaiah discovered.

Preaching has a hard edge to it that exposes spiritual darkness, and makes people feel very uncomfortable. The best preaching is 'straight talking', not relying on rhetoric, but the direct challenge of the word of God. Micaiah's story also reminds us that true, biblical preachers are in the minority. They stand against the prevailing culture. The false prophets surrounding Ahab's court, telling him what he wanted to hear, were in the majority. It can feel very lonely being a faithful, challenging Bible teacher, swimming against the tide of popular opinion, but power and truth will follow you when you declare the undiluted word of God.

Revelation versus exposition

One very important point to make is that preachers today are not in the same position as Old Testament prophets. God gave these prophets direct words of revelation to communicate. The prophets were 'inspired' in a way that modern preachers are not.

Our job is to preach what the prophets and apostles have recorded in Scripture for us. We are not to sit in our study on a Saturday night and wait for a 'word from heaven' for our hearers, while our Bible gathers dust on the shelf. Our task is exposition, not revelation — exposing the truth of what has already been revealed in the word of God. Indeed, it can be very dangerous when a pastor today believes himself to be an inspired prophet like Isaiah or Jeremiah.

There are many churches where preachers 'prophesy' rather than preach. They feel they have an inspired 'word from the Lord', so they do not do the hard work of studying a Bible passage, but instead pass on what they feel the Lord has spoken to them. That is a very dangerous approach.

Many things have been said in Jesus' name that are not the word of God and do damage to his church. Of course, there is a place for prophetic words in our churches but those words need to be 'weighed' carefully by godly leaders in the church to test if they are from God or not (see 1 Jn. 4: 1—3). It is tempting for a pastor to abuse his power, claiming visions and prophetic words from

God that God has never said, and commanding people to obey. The Micaiah story reminds us that false spirits can also be at work in prophesying, and Satan loves it when leaders use the name of God for their own advantage.

Prophetic words should never replace the week-by-week exposition of passages from the word of God. Preaching a Bible text keeps the preacher accountable for correctly delivering the word of God so that people can recognize when a preacher has strayed from the pure teaching of the Word. The book of Acts tells us about the Bereans who, after listening to Paul preach, carefully examined the scriptures to see if what Paul was saying was true (Acts 17: 11). That is a very healthy process, and even the great apostle needed to have his teaching assessed according to biblical truth. Keeping the Bible, rather than the latest 'inspired word' at the centre of our churches, will keep us from error.

New Testament Preaching

When we come to the New Testament, we need to consider the preaching of Jesus himself. Preaching was a priority to Jesus, even more than healing. He did both wonderfully of course, but when people were crowding him, wanting to see his latest miracle, he said, 'Let us go somewhere else—to the nearby villages—so I can preach there also. That is why I have come' (Mark 1: 38).

Preaching must also be a priority for modern pastors and leaders. It is tempting to fill your life with committee meetings, pastoral contacts, and setting out vision for your church while time for preaching is neglected. But we do our best leading from the pulpit. And it becomes very noticeable when a preacher stops putting in the hours of study and prayer required to produce powerful, clear, Bible-based messages. If you are a regular preacher, give your best hours to preaching preparation, and give away other roles and tasks to trusted workers.

What is noteworthy about Jesus' preaching was his desire to speak to ordinary men and women. He used everyday illustrations—farmers sowing seeds in their fields, widows seeking justice from a local judge, a son being reckless with his father's inheritance. Jesus became popular among poor, uneducated fisher folk because he spoke in a language they could relate to, rather than using academic, flowery words that no one could understand.

And like Old Testament prophets, Jesus did not mince his words. He called Pharisees 'snakes' (Mt.23: 33) and King Herod, a 'fox' (Lk.13: 32). His preaching searched the deepest motives of the human heart. The Sermon on the Mount (Matt. 5—7) delves into issues like lust, spiritual hypocrisy, the love of money, and the arrogance of false teachers. Jesus constantly hit 'raw nerves' with a direct and uncompromising style.

Similarly our job as preachers is not be fine orators who talk about empty theories, using formal rhetoric. Our God-given task is to unleash the power of God's truth, like a sword, into peoples' hearts, uncovering sinful motives, cleaning out the weeds they would sooner cover up, until they have been washed by the Word (Eph. 5: 26). You cannot have a proper wash until you have been stripped bare, and the Scriptures are God's scalpel which he wields to open our souls, not for our destruction, but our salvation.

Paul and the Apostles

When we come to the preaching of Paul and the apostles, we realize their dominant theme was Christ and the salvation he brought. Paul said to the Corinthians, who were looking for more entertaining preaching, 'I resolved to know nothing among you except Jesus Christ and him crucified' (1 Cor. 2: 2). He was so focused on Christ's death and resurrection that scholars are puzzled about why he said so little about Jesus' teaching.

All nine sermons in the book of Acts speak about the salvation Christ brings, mentioning the resurrection nine times, and the cross eight times. While the Bible is full of themes we can talk about, our core message is salvation through Jesus Christ, calling men and women to 'repent and believe the Gospel' (Acts 2: 38). And even mature Christians need to keep hearing the message of the cross, so that we live in the light of God's grace every day and keep coming back to the core of our faith.

The two great ordinances of the church—baptism and communion—both focus, not on the teachings of Christ, but on his cross as the heartbeat of Christian belief. So our preaching should never stray far from the culmination of God's plan of salvation, where his Son died for our sins and rose again on the third day (1 Cor. 15: 1-5). Even when you are preaching a series from an Old Testament book, always relate that teaching to the Gospel and the cross.

Remember that Jesus, on the road to Emmaus showed how the Old Testament ultimately pointed to his coming as Messiah, and the death he had to die for sin (Luke 24: 27). Never move far away from the Gospel.

What is also clear from the apostles' preaching was that the Bible can be preached in many different settings. Paul spoke in churches on Sunday, but he also preached in Athens city centre (Acts 17: 16-34), by a river bank in Philippi (Acts 16: 13), and he even hired a lecture hall to debate with Jews about Jesus the Messiah (Acts 19: 9).

The apostle Peter tells us to take every opportunity presented to us to make known the Word. Don't wait for people to sit in pews before you preach to them. Take the Word out to where people are — to the 'marketplace'— whatever that looks like in your context. Some of the most fruitful preaching in the UK takes place in pubs in the middle of the week, at lunchtimes in local businesses and on University campuses. The vast majority of Jesus' preaching was not in the synagogue but on mountainsides and by Lake Galilee. Don't be rigid about where you can bring the word of God!

The importance of preaching

Paul is also at pains to show that preaching was God's chosen method of communication:

> For Christ did not send me to baptize but to *preach* the
> Gospel…the *message* of the cross is foolishness to those who
> are perishing, but to us who are being saved it is the power
> of God…For…God was pleased through the foolishness of
> what was *preached* to save those who believe….we *preach*
> Christ crucified.
> (1 Cor. 1:17-23, emphasis mine).

Many people today, in our audio/visual age, doubt the value of preaching. They say we need to tell more stories or form discussion groups. All those have their place in Gospel communication, but it is clear from Paul's words that preaching was God's primary chosen means of bringing the message of Christ to men and women.

The main word for preaching in the New Testament is the Greek word 'kerusso' which means to 'herald' or 'proclaim'. It is a bit like a town crier in ancient times announcing the command of the King in towns and villages across England. The message is not open to debate. It is a command of God who 'calls all people everywhere to repent' (Acts 17.30).

There is real authority in a preacher declaring the word of God, which we must never lose. Truth is relative to most people today, in the West at least. We prefer discussion groups where we can share our opinions. But there comes a time when we need to hear the authoritative Word of the Lord, proclaimed with boldness. This message is not open to opinion or negotiation. It is the command of God, presented through his human mouthpiece.

The Early Church (30-499 AD)

Many Christians view the early church as a golden era. Men and women were willing to die for their faith, as the message spread far and wide. But this was not a good time for Biblical preaching.

Many of the preachers and teachers of the early church, such as Origen and Jerome, had strange methods of interpreting the Bible. They allegorized much of Scripture in such a way that they did not deal with the plain meaning of the biblical text, but were always looking for deeper interpretations and pictures that lost the impact of the text.

Augustine (354—430 AD) was the first scholar to attempt real Bible exposition, and he produced over 600 sermons, among which were expositions of the Psalms, the Gospels and 1 John. But the preacher who had the most impact in this era was John Chrysostom (349 – 457 AD). He was nicknamed 'golden mouthed' because of the power of his preaching. Chrysostom preached verse-by-verse and passage-by-passage Bible expositions (precisely the kind of preaching we are proposing in this book) on many Bible books including Genesis, Psalms, Matthew, Romans and several letters of Paul.

Although Chrysostom was a gifted orator, he did not rely on rhetoric. He was known for simple Bible exposition, for boldly challenging the loose morals of his listeners, and for applying the Bible text directly to ordinary men and women, just as Jesus and the prophets had done. Crowds flocked to hear him preach and the church historian Philip Schaff described him as one of 'the greatest pulpit orators of the Greek church'.[3] There was a real power when people were confronted boldly with the plain teaching of the Bible text.

The Mediaeval Period (500-1499)

During the mediaeval period the church generally moved away from a Bible-centred faith. The authority of the church seemed to supersede the authority of the Bible, so that what the Pope or bishops said became of equal importance with what Scripture taught.

There were a couple of well-known preachers during this time, not least Thomas Aquinas, and Bernard of Clairvaux who was instrumental in the Crusades. Both these men were noteworthy theologians and godly men but again they did not handle the Bible text in an expository fashion. Allegorical interpretations ruled the day and the plain, direct, verse-by-verse teaching of a Chrysostom was sadly lacking.

Perhaps related to the lack of Bible-centredness, the church moved away from core doctrines of Scripture and began to promote doctrines like purgatory which have no grounding in Scripture but allowed an increasingly corrupt church to manipulate members to pay their way out of purgatory and add to the wealth of the church. Praying to saints became important, as did the elevation of Mary, mother of Jesus. Masses were spoken mostly in Latin, a language which the ordinary man did not understand, and this 'mindless' ceremony took centre stage while Bible exposition was almost non-existent.

It was this sorry state of affairs that prompted men like John Wycliffe (1330 – 1384) and William Tyndale (c.1494 – 1536) in England, and Jan Hus (c.1369) – 1415) in Prague to challenge church authority. Wycliffe, in particular, denounced the preaching of his day, saying that any sermon that did not deal with Scripture should be rejected. His dream was that every man, woman and child should have a copy of the Scriptures available to them in a language they could understand.

---

3 P. Schaff, *History of the Christian Church*, 8 vols. 18ch. 7, section 90. Oak Harbor, WA: Logos Research Systems, Inc. 1997.

Over in Bohemia, Jan Hus began preaching bold Bible messages which impacted a great number of Czech students and little by little a 'back to the Bible' movement began which was to be the seedbed of the Protestant Reformation.

The Reformation (1500-1599)

Few have impacted the cause of biblical preaching like Martin Luther (1483 – 1546). His own conversion story, where he discovered, through a close study of Romans 1: 17, that righteousness was a gift from God, reveals how much paying close attention to Scripture set the agenda for the Reformation.

Luther's whole complaint in the 95 theses (arguments) that he famously nailed to the door of All Saints' Church, Wittenberg, was that the church of his day had moved so far away from the moorings of Scripture that they had lost the central message of the Bible. That central message was salvation, not by good works or religious ritual, but, the Reformers argued, 'by grace alone, through faith alone, in Christ alone'.

Luther shared Wycliffe's dream of having Scripture available to everyone, and, by God's providence, technical advancements in printing meant that suddenly the Bible became available to regular people, and so the thirst for the kind of preaching that explained the Bible clearly became almost overwhelming across Europe.

Luther famously said, 'the Word comes first, and with the Word the Spirit breathes upon my heart so that I believe'[4] . He produced commentaries on Genesis, Psalms, Romans, Galatians and Hebrews and preached sermon series on the Gospels and Paul's Epistles. Perhaps his most famous quote, having turned Europe and church history upside down by his bullish determination, was 'I simply taught, preached, wrote God's Word: otherwise I did nothing… The Word did it all.' (Timothy George, 'Theology of Reformers', Broadman & Holman; 25th Revised edition edition, 2013, p.53).

If Luther was the bulldog of the Reformation, John Calvin (1509 – 1564), a quiet, sensitive genius, was its chief theologian. His commitment to preaching is summed up not just by his prodigious output (he preached every day for years, verse-by-verse), but also by his definition of the task of a Gospel minister.

---

4 M. Luther, *Table Talk* Fortress Press 1967, no.402.

In his *Institutes* he said of ministers, 'their whole task is limited to the ministry of God's Word, their whole wisdom to the knowledge of his Word: their whole eloquence to its proclamation'.[5]

Calvin was such a good writer, it is better to describe his approach to preaching in his own words. Speaking of the preacher he said:

> Since it is almost his only task to unfold the mind of the
> (Bible) writer whom he has undertaken to expound, he misses
> his mark, or at least strays outside the limits, by the extent
> to which he leads his readers away from the meaning of his
> author.[6]

And so, with these convictions coursing through his veins, Calvin spent his life preaching the Bible, passage-by-passage, book-by-book and left behind him one of the most powerful legacies of church history. With the city of Geneva as his base, Calvin preached twice each Sunday and every weekday on alternating weeks from 1549 until his death in 1564. This included three years preaching through Isaiah.

The Puritans (1600-1699)

If the Reformation lit a spark for truly biblical preaching, the Puritans fanned that spark into a flame. The Puritans emphasized preaching so much that they moved their pulpits from the sides of their churches to the centre. For centuries of Roman Catholic Christianity, the altar had taken centre stage, and the mass had replaced the Bible as the means of salvation.

The Puritans went the other way. Their churches were often very bland with no stained-glass windows or altars. They even banned musical instruments so that nothing would take the mind away from hearing the word of God preached. Their conviction is summed up best by Martin Lloyd Jones, 'the exposition of the word of God…must control everything.'[7]

---

5 Ernie Klassen, *Revival Preaching,* Lulu Publishing Services 2016), p.48

6 David L. Puckett, *John Calvin's Exegesis of the Old Testament,* Westminster John Knox Press, 1995, p.13

7 D. M. Lloyd-Jones, *The Puritans: their origins and successors,* Edinburgh: Banner of Truth 1987, p.378.

William Perkins (1558 – 1602) was a prime mover among the Puritans and his instructions to preachers identify 4 principles of true, expository preaching:

1. To read the text distinctly out of the Scriptures
2. To give the sense and understanding of it, being read, by the Scripture itself
3. To collect a few and profitable points of doctrine out of the natural sense (of the passage)
4. To apply the doctrines, rightly collected, to the life and manner of men in a simple and plain speech[8]

What strikes you about the Puritan preachers is that God used all of them, with their unique styles and personalities. Here is how John Brown described three great puritan preachers of his era:

> (John) Owen preached earnestly to the understanding, reasoning from his critical and devout knowledge of Scripture; (Richard) Baxter preached forcibly to the conscience … while (Thomas) Goodwin appealed to the affections … interpreting Scripture by the insight of a renewed heart.[9]

The best preachers are not those who copy others in the pulpit but use the gifts and personality God has given them. 'Be yourself' in the pulpit is a key insight from the Puritan period.

The Evangelicals (the 1700s)

George Whitefield (1714 – 1770) is arguably the best preacher from church history. Crowds of up to 70,000 used to gather to hear him preach in the open air. He had to preach in fields because he was thrown out of the sleepy Anglican churches of his day who found his style too zealous for their liking.

When you preach the Bible, don't speak as if it were a lecture purely on the content of Scripture. The role of the preacher is to inspire an encounter

---

8 Michael Duduit, editor, *Handbook of Contemporary Preaching*, Broadman Press, 1992, p.96

9 John Brown, *Puritan Preaching in England: a Study of Past and Present*, Ulan Press, 2012), p.72

between the listener and the living God. Passion must flame from your heart, or you have no business declaring the living oracles of God.

Whitefield's passionate preaching brought revival to both east coast America, and much of the UK. Pubs were emptied, churches were crowded, and many were so overwhelmed by the power and presence of the Holy Spirit that they fainted and needed to be removed from the meetings. Those days of revival were very special, and cannot be repeated on a whim, but it is a reminder that every preacher is utterly dependent on the power of the Holy Spirit to bring about real change in peoples' hearts.

What is often missing from preachers today is not sound doctrine, or skill in putting a message together, but the kind of prayer that casts preachers on God and acknowledges that nothing of eternal value can be achieved without the power of the Holy Spirit. Whitefield, and his close colleague John Wesley (1703 – 1791) travelled thousands of miles on horseback, bringing passionate Gospel-driven preaching to all parts of the UK and America and lit revival fire such as had not been seen since the days of the Apostles.

The Modern Era (1800-today)

Nothing has done more to damage the cause of biblical preaching than the rise of Protestant liberalism. The 1800s saw such an increase in scientific knowledge and criticism of the Bible text in academic circles, that many Christians lost their confidence in the miracles of the Bible. These so-called Christians still wanted the community side of church but undermined the authority of Scripture, and their false teaching is still wreaking havoc today.

Liberalism wants a faith without the 'hard edges' of the Bible: the miracles which are hard to accept in a scientific age; the moral values of the Bible that sit uncomfortably with the ever changing morals of society today; and perhaps most especially the doctrines of wrath and judgement that are so unpopular.

Liberalism is the fulfilment of Paul's prediction to Timothy:

> For the time will come when people will not put up with sound doctrine. Instead to suit their own desires, they will gather around them a great number of teachers to say what their itching ears want to hear.
> (2 Tim. 4: 3—4)

This is the battle we face today more strongly than ever. The battle to keep the Bible at the centre of our churches and to preach 'the truth, the whole truth and nothing but the truth, so help us God'. This is a battle that men and women have died for throughout church history. Every generation of Bible preachers *must* keep speaking the truth, no matter what pressures culture puts on us. The word of God *must* be unleashed to speak into the darkness of each generation. If it is not, the church becomes irrelevant. If it is, the demons tremble!

CHAPTER 3

Deaf ears: why people don't want to hear

Stephen McQuoid

I always feel a little nervous when I preach. This is not because I lack experience, on the contrary I have been preaching regularly for over 30 years. However, the importance of the task and the pressure of standing up in front of other people means that preaching is always a slightly uncomfortable experience. Only once, however, have I felt really intimidated when preaching. I was at a church in London and the passage I was asked to preach on was Romans 1. This great chapter deals with the weighty issue of God's judgment. I tried to expound the text faithfully when someone in the audience interrupted me and publicly criticized me for what I was saying. It was a difficult situation to handle and made me feel very vulnerable in the pulpit. However, it was also an important reminder that preaching is not always popular among those who listen.

My experience was one that some of the great preachers of the Bible would have been able to identify with. Men like Amos, Isaiah, Ezekiel and the apostle Paul had a great deal of opposition to their preaching and it took great courage for each of them to faithfully declare the message that God had given them. There were, of course, different reasons for the opposition that they faced but it made the job of preaching a difficult one for each of them. History has moved on but something that has never changed is the resistance that some people have towards preaching. In today's world there are many reasons why contemporary audiences will find good, biblical preaching unpalatable.

The IT generation

One of the first reasons why many people struggle to listen to good preaching is that we live in a world that is saturated with media (especially social media) and information technology. Indeed, there has never been a time in all of human history like the present, where the preacher has had to deal with an audience so accustomed to sound bites, fake news and instant images that are available at the push of a button.

Forty years ago when I was a child, televisions were a status symbol and most, but by no means all, households had one. Today it is not hard to find households with several tvs, a DVD, a Blu-ray, a sophisticated stereo system, wifi, laptops, tablets, hand-held devices and a dizzying range of computer games. This technology is, of course, a real blessing and can be used positively to enhance people's lives. However, there is also a downside. We now live in a society where many people have a remarkably short attention span and an insatiable desire for the instant and the easily accessible. Social media has conditioned us to be more interested in voyeurism and the trite, rather than thinking hard about the truly big issues that affect our world. The sheer speed of our televisual world can be seen when we look at television commercials. Most commercials last for only about half a minute yet are full of activity as camera angles change every few seconds and the message is given in brief sound bites.

How does this media saturation affect people today and why does this make preaching a challenge? Firstly there is the simple issue of concentration. If people have become so used to rapidly changing images and the instant accessibility of information then sitting through a sermon which is essentially a monologue is hard work. It takes effort to engage with what is being said and that is something many are not prepared to do, at least not for any length of time. I can remember being invited by one church to preach on Romans 5. I was staggered to discover that they expected me to cover the passage in 8 minutes and when I asked why I had so little time to preach they said that they felt people would not be able to concentrate for much longer than that.

Often this lack of concentration is accompanied by an uncritical attitude that can also develop as a result of media saturation. Television has great educational value, but most of the time it is used for entertainment. This in itself is not wrong but viewers can be so used to being in entertainment mode that they are not used to really thinking hard about an issue as it takes too much effort. Preaching is not entertaining. The preacher is trying to grapple with the text and enable the reader to understand what the passage is saying. Again this takes effort as the listener has to reflect on what is being said and this is alien to people who are more used to just watching something because it is fun.

There is also the issue of the kind of communication involved in preaching. Some preachers are very absorbing because they are very charismatic personalities but this is not universally true. There can be variety and drama in preaching but the preacher still needs to compete with music, computer games, TV sitcoms and comedies and they are media of communication that are more colourful and fascinating than someone just speaking. All of these challenges make the job of preaching in our contemporary society a difficult one.

Individualism

Another issue the preacher faces is the individualism that is present in many cultures and societies. Many people, particularly in the West, are used to having a great deal of personal freedom to do what they want. Their autonomy is seen as a virtue and people who conform to political, moral or religious systems are sneered at and perceived to be weak and imprisoned. This kind of individualism breeds an attitude that says, 'You can't tell me what to do or what to believe'. Indeed, anyone who does try to make demands is treated with suspicion and hostility.

Again this attitude makes the job of preaching very difficult. Preachers are not in the business of negotiating. They are not telling their audiences that they can just pick and choose which parts of the sermon they want to obey and which parts they can disregard. Preachers are not in the business of being ambiguous or giving their audience the impression that the content of their sermons is unimportant. On the contrary, the job of the preacher is to tell people what God is saying and to demand obedience.

True preaching is biblical. It looks at the teaching and requirements of Scripture and communicates this to the listeners with the conviction that this is the word of God and it must be obeyed. Everyone including the preacher falls under the authority of the Bible. He does not have the right to tone down what the Bible says or express it in such a way that makes it more palatable. The preacher is simply God's mouthpiece declaring to people what God wants them to hear.

This will, of course, mean that the preaching of the word of God will come up against the desire that people in the audience will have for self-determination. When a person is listening to preaching there is a decision to be made. He or she can either live as they please or they can choose to obey God. This will be a tough decision to make in any culture, but in a culture where individualism is prominent and people are used to making decisions for their own lives and reticent to listen to others, the battle is even greater. In such situations people must dethrone their egos and surrender their wills to God. Some will do this, others will resist and that will make the job of preaching difficult.

Concept of truth

Another challenge that preaching faces is the concept of truth that exists in many cultures. Postmodern relativism has had an impact globally, especially among young people and has led to a belief that truth is a fairly arbitrary thing. There are scientific and mathematical facts that are accepted as true in an absolute sense but any other truth-claims are seen as nothing more than personal opinion. If someone argues for a religious truth-claim or tries to defend a particular ethical position they may be listened to, but their claims are viewed as nothing more than personal opinion, certainly not something to be considered objectively true. This way of viewing truth makes all truth claims equally valid even if they contradict one another. One person might say, 'There is only one god and his name is Allah'; another might say, 'There is no god' and still another might say, 'There are many gods'. According to postmodern relativism each person is expressing a personal opinion and no one can say that his statement is true in any exclusive or absolute sense. In essence when this worldview becomes the norm then everything is true and nothing is true.

This attitude to truth comes into direct conflict with the Christian faith and Christian preaching. For Christians the truth of the word of God is absolute and irrevocable. The Bible does not express an opinion or a perspective on a variety of issue: what it says is true! It is not just true for some people, it is universally true for all people in every culture. Even if some people refuse to believe the Bible and angrily claim it is false. it remains true and their opinion of it cannot diminish this.

Christian preaching is the declaration of the truth of the Bible. As long as the preacher is declaring what the word of God says then he declares truth. If the concept of truth in any given cultural setting means that all truth claims are brought into question and relegated to the realm of personal opinion, then it is not the Bible or the preaching of the Bible that is at fault, but rather the culture itself. The end result is a clash between Christian preaching which openly states that the Bible is absolutely true and a culture that resists the very notion of objective truth. Preaching in this kind of environment is inevitably going to be a challenge.

The instant word

Over the past few decades there has been a resurgence in the use of spiritual gifts in the life of the church and this has brought blessing, growth and encouragement. However as with many situations, the potential for imbalance, abuse and extremes has also been present. Some churches have been guilty of over-emphasizing some gifts at the expense of others which is exactly the problem that prompted Paul to write his first Epistle to the Corinthians. This does not lead to a healthy church life so when this problem arises it should be redressed.

One of the most neglected gifts in many churches is that of preaching. Sadly, many of these churches have preferred to have the instant word from God in the form of prophecy rather than listening to Biblical preaching. This has meant that preaching has had to take second place. Preaching may take a lot of preparation and also discipline on the part of those who listen but it needs to be part of the staple diet of any church so that Christians can learn, be inspired, be challenged and build up a biblical worldview. That is not to say that prophecy is wrong, on the contrary it too has a role to play. However, it must be balanced with the preaching of the word of God.

Marginalization of the Sermon in Church Life

Yet another obstacle which preaching faces in contemporary church life is the marginalization of the sermon in the church programme. This is probably not a deliberate thing and in reality, very few churches want to dispense with preaching altogether. Almost all would say that preaching is important, but the credibility of this claim is often tested when any given church programme is being put together.

There has been a huge drive in recent years to make church appealing and accessible. This of course is a good thing because no one wants church to be boring and it certainly does not honour God when we put no thought into how we conduct the life of our churches. However, in an attempt to make church appealing, many churches have opted for a church service format that focuses on enjoyment and activity at the expense of content and meaning.

Churches will have quizzes and drama, children's slot, puppetry, video clips and interactive activities, and lots of worship, all of which are good and have their place. The problem is that church programmes get so crowded that the thing which suffers and ends up being marginalised is the sermon. While this may not be deliberate, it is deadly. Rather than making the sermon the central point of a church service it becomes a brief appendix at the end. It is almost as if we want to make so much noise that we drown out the voice of God. This is a problem because in such an atmosphere the preaching of the word of God loses its authority and impact and becomes little more than a side show.

The monster of laziness

So far we have looked at the many obstacles that get in the way of preaching and make the preacher's job a difficult one. However, there is one more obstacle that needs to be considered and it is one that particularly affects the preacher himself as he tries to prepare for his sermon. That is the obstacle of laziness.

Good preaching is the result of very hard work. Someone once said that preaching is five percent inspiration and ninety five percent perspiration. There is real truth in this. To deliver a good sermon takes real discipline and perseverance. The preacher firstly has to thoroughly grasp the meaning of the text. Anyone who has read the Bible in detail will know this is hard work. Then there is the issue of application. The preacher needs to think about how this passage should speak to his audience. Once this is done there is the issue of presentation and how all of this can best be communicated. Finally, there is practice as the content of the message is absorbed and in the preacher's mind so that the preaching can flow.

All of this takes time and effort. The problem is that many preachers are tempted to take shortcuts, not least because church life can be very pressurized. Preparing little and preaching light has often been considered an option — it is not! The long-term effect will be congregations that do not know their Bibles and are not challenged to live holy lives. The preacher must fight the temptation to be lazy so he can serve God and the congregation well through good preaching.

CHAPTER 4

Covering the distance:
The challenge of reading ancient texts

Stephen McQuoid

I was sitting at gate number 6 at Dubai International Airport waiting to board a plane bound for Seoul in South Korea. The fascination I once had with airports had long since receded simply because I have been through so many of them as a result of my job. My method of coping with the boredom of all the waiting was to have a good book with me which I read with interest. Opposite me on the neat rows of chairs by the gate was an elderly Pakistani gentleman with his wife. We smiled at each other and exchanged glances. The book in my hands had a dramatic front cover so intrigued the gentleman that he asked me what it was. As it happened it was a book on the history of western philosophy. The expression of his face immediately showed disinterest. Though he smiled once more just to be polite, 'I don't read' he said. Then he picked up a newspaper and proceeded to do just what he denied doing —he read it.

The truth is that just about all of us read whether it is books, newspapers, comic books, instruction manuals for our car or washing machine or simply the free averts that get thrust through our letterboxes. What many people don't do, however, is read carefully and read in a way that demonstrates what kind of thing they are reading. This is because almost all of our reading is casual.

When it comes to preaching, the preacher must first of all understand the passage he is to speak from and that requires him to have read and understood it properly. After all, how can he speak with any authority about the passage if he really doesn't know what it is about? This will involve learning to carefully read and understand the Bible.

Learning how to read the Bible properly is a discipline that can take a lifetime to really master. Commentaries and Bible study aids are invaluable but all too often we turn to them far too quickly and avoid the really hard work of wrestling with Scripture. I once told a student off in a class I was teaching on the book of Amos. He was unfamiliar with the book so when he was asked to produce some work on chapter 5, he went first to a commentary on the book of Amos and having read that he then turned to chapter 5 to read it. This was a mistake as no commentary however brilliant can ever replace just sitting with the Bible in hand and reading it carefully.

While mastering the Bible takes a lifetime, learning to read it properly is actually fairly simple and obvious. Indeed the starting point is just simply learning to read and pay attention to important details. This comes naturally if we love the Bible and value it. When I first met my wife and we began a relationship, we were actually living in two different countries and so we wrote to each other. When her letters arrived I read them carefully and over and over again because I wanted to really grasp what she was saying. Reading the Bible in this way will help us to see the important details.

Repetition

The very first thing we should notice as we read any passage is the repetition of words. Every word is a vehicle that conveys meaning. As we read a passage our brain instinctively picks out the words that are significant. When these words are repeated several times within just a few sentences you know that you are onto something. An obvious example of this is 1 John 2:15-17. As you read these verses you can't help but notice that the word 'world' is mentioned no less than six times. We are told not to love the world or anything in the world. John is obviously very much concerned with the 'world'. Consequently, we can only really understand this passage if we grasp the significance of John's use of the word 'world'.

Lists

Similarly we should notice any lists that are used for they too highlight something significant that is being said. Lists are particularly common in the New Testament epistles as they fit naturally into this kind of literature. Galatians 5:22-23 is an example of this. Paul is trying to articulate the kind of changes that take place in a person's life if they are under the influence of the Holy Spirit. He gives us a list of these spiritual qualities which he calls the 'fruit of the Spirit' and it is self-evident that we are not just to rush past this list but rather look at each word carefully and ask what it tells us about the Christian life.

Contrasts

Another thing to look out for is contrasts. Something is said and then its opposite is mentioned. The book of Proverbs is one where lots of contrasts are mentioned. Each time there is something important to say it is because the writer is contrasting two kinds of lifestyle. In Proverbs 15:1 we are told that *gentle answers turn away wrath but a harsh word stirs up anger.* Practical experience tells us that frequently this happens — it is true to life — and the wisdom of the writer of Proverbs is clearly seen. His wisdom is couched in the contrast that is drawn. A similar contrast can be seen in Psalm 1 where the lifestyle in the first three verses is contrasted with the lifestyle in verses four and five.

Comparison

The opposite of a contrast is a comparison and there are plenty of these in the Bible too. They perform the same function in that they draw our attention to what the writer wants to say. The thing that is being used as a comparison adds real richness to our understanding. One of the most famous comparisons is found in Isaiah 40:31. Here the person who *waits on the Lord* is being compared to an eagle. I live in Scotland and love climbing mountains in the Highlands. One of the most spectacular sights is the mighty and majestic golden eagle gliding effortlessly above the mountains. The sheer beauty and calm of their flight provides a perfect picture of the impact that God can have on our lives as we wait on him.

Figures of speech

Look also for figures of speech which are an important device that lots of biblical writers use. A figure of speech is a literary device in which words are used in a sense that is other than the normal. This too is a way of getting the reader to focus on a point that the writer is trying to highlight. Take for example the well-known verse Psalm 119:105 *Your word is a lamp for my feet and a light for my path*. God's word is not literally a lamp. However, we all know what a lamp does. If you are out in the countryside far away from the lights of a busy city and the sun goes down, walking suddenly becomes dangerous because you can't see where you are going or see any hazards in the way. A lamp, however, would be able to illuminate the path before you and therefore you could walk in safety. The psalmist uses this figure of speech to demonstrate the great importance of using the word of God as a guide for our lives.

Conjunctions

Slightly more difficult to spot but still important are conjunctions. These are joining words that put the major components of a sentence together. If I could use an analogy, it is as if I was building a brick wall. The cement that holds the bricks together would play the same role that a conjunction does in a sentence. When we talk about conjunctions we are talking about words like 'and, therefore, because, since, but'. Very often you can make sense of an entire book and see its structure if you pay attention to the conjunctions. The book of Romans is a very good example of this. Romans 12:1 says *Therefore I urge you, brothers and sisters, in view of God's mercy, to offer your bodies as a living sacrifice* (Rom. 12: 1). The conjunction '*therefore*' is at the start of this verse and that is very significant. What Paul is saying is that our bodies should be given as living sacrifices because of what he has said earlier in the book. In previous chapters he has explained to the Christians in Rome the mystery of the gospel and as a result of this they should live surrendered lives. If you read through Romans you will see the word 'therefore' appearing throughout and its regular appearance helps you to see the whole thought flow of the book.

Verbs

Of course, conjunctions are not the only words you should look out for. Verbs are also crucial. Verbs are doing words. They are words that tell us what is happening; they are the action words that denote activity. When you see a verb it is always good to ask if the action being described is past, present or future or whether it is an imperative verb, that is a command, such as the one Jesus gives in Matthew 28:18 to *Go into all the world*. The verb will take you to the very heart of what the writer is saying. There is a good example in Matthew 6:19 where Jesus tells the crowd not to store up treasures on earth but to store them up in heaven.

Cause and effect

One final thing that you should note when reading any passage is the presence of cause and effect. Every action will have a reaction and this relationship should always be identified. In the Bible there are good and bad examples of cause and effect. At times when bad actions take place the effect is also bad (often God's judgment). But we also read of good actions which have a good effect. There are even verses where both good and bad appear together, as in Romans 6:23 where the cause of sin leads to the effect of death and the cause of God's giving leads to the effect of eternal life.

Careful reading of an ancient text

Reading carefully is obviously very important. Remember that as a preacher you have the important task of grasping what the word of God says so that you can convey this to the people to whom you are preaching. Consequently, preachers need to work very hard at understanding the text. It must be stated however that reading the Bible is not like reading a contemporary novel or a newspaper or magazine. This is because while careful reading is done in the same way as it would be in any literature, the Bible has the added complication of being a library of ancient books. What is more these books are set in very different geographical and cultural locations from the one we live in. This means that we also need to think about the issue of distance, that is, the distance between us and the world in which these ancient texts emerged. If we do not keep this distance in mind, we will end up making some fairly basic mistakes.

Modern Assumptions

To illustrate this, a colleague of mine was recently in Kenya doing some training with a group of young church leaders who were learning to preach. They each had to study a passage and then preach a sermon to the rest of the group. One of these students was given Luke 5 to preach on which tells the story of Jesus by the Lake of Gennesaret. In this story Jesus climbed into Simon's boat; had the boat pushed out a little into the water and then sat in it to preach to the crowds. As the student delivered his sermon, he asked the question, why did Jesus get into a boat and preach a distance from the shore?

Answering his own question, he went on to say that if you go to a beach you will find people scantily clad and lying in the sun which would have been a distraction to the people trying to listen to Jesus. Of course, this conclusion was just an assumption on the part of the student, not something you would find in the text. However, it shows the issue of distance in time, culture and geography. If you go to a private beach in Mombasa, you would indeed see swimmers lying in the sun in their swimwear. Two thousand years ago in rural Palestine it would not have been culturally acceptable for this to have happened. Without a proper closing of the distance between the young preacher and the text, misunderstandings were bound to happen. We will read our own assumptions into the text rather than accurately listening to it.

Translations

As we read bible passages closely, we need to remind ourselves that we are reading a translation and that the Bible is written primarily in Hebrew and Greek. No one translation will be perfect and different translations do their work in different ways. Some, for example, will do their best to translate a passage word for word. Others get the general sense of a sentence and find the best words that can express the meaning, and this is called using 'dynamic equivalence'. No one way is better than another; however, it is a good practice to use several bible versions when preparing a sermon as that is the best guarantee of accuracy.

Historical context

The next thing we face is the distance that comes from the historical context. There are actually three aspects to this historical context.

Authors

Firstly, there is the author who has written the book. God choose to use ordinary humans to write the Bible. They were not treated as if they were robots or mechanical dictaphones. They were real people with their own personal history and cultural values. They even had different levels of education and sophistication which show up in their writing. Luke was educated and his gospel is very polished. John was a deep thinker and his writings appear to be a little mystical.

Life stories

Who the writers were is important when it comes to really grasping what they say. For example, in Philippians 3:8 Paul refers to his former life and declares it *garbage*; that he *considers everything a loss because of the surpassing worth of knowing Christ*. When you realise that Paul was a deeply devout Jew, a Pharisee who rigidly adhered to the Law as he believed it would make him right with God, then you begin to grasp just how significant this statement is.

Audience

As well as the writer, there is an issue about the audience. The Bible is an old book and was written to people whose whole world view was tied up in the ancient world and within a given cultural setting. Modern readers might wonder why Matthews's gospel begins with a long list of names until they realise that the Jewish audience for whom Matthew was writing saw huge significance in genealogies. Jeremiah also wrote those beautiful words *"For I know the plans I have for you," declares the* Lord, *"plans to prosper you and not to harm you, plans to give you hope and a future"* (Jeremiah 29:11). These words take on a whole new meaning when you realise that the original audience were experiencing God's discipline in exile.

Historical or cultural elements

Historical and cultural elements are also important. This might include, for example, the geography of the country. The New Testament often speaks of people going 'up' to Jerusalem (Acts 21: 12) or 'down' to Jericho (Luke 10: 30). A quick look at a biblical atlas reveals why. It might also include social customs such as the kinsman-redeemer that we encounter in the book of Ruth where Boaz is able to preserve the family name by providing an heir for Naomi's two dead sons by marrying Ruth. Economic issues might feature. Take the story of Paul casting out an evil spirit from a slave girl in Philippi (Acts 16:16—24). Her owners, far from being pleased with the help they had given, had them beaten and jailed because of the loss of income they incurred because the girl was no longer able to work as a fortune teller. There could be some important legal details that affect the text such as the prohibition on the public punishing of Roman citizens without a trial (Acts 16: 37). Each of these wider cultural elements distances us from the text and need to be dealt with.

Interpretation

Once all of this is done, how do we actually go about reading the text and making a proper interpretation? There are essentially four steps that we have to go through. The first step is to ask what the text meant to the audience? Look at all the clues in the text and gather together all the information you know about the setting and think through what that audience would make of what was written.

The second step is to ascertain what distances are involved in making this interpretation. In other words, what are the cultural, linguistic and geographical factors that we need to consider in order to understand this passage in its proper context?

Thirdly we need to extrapolate a theological principle from what we know in the text. We have observed what it says, but what does it actually *mean*? The passage is trying to teach us something, but what *is* it trying to teach us? When Amos told the worshippers to get rid of their singing and music and that God would not listen to their praises (Amos 5: 23), he was not actually banning all worship, but he was saying something very important about the kind of worship God finds acceptable.

The fourth stage is to ask how the biblical text applies to contemporary audiences. Clearly lots of the customs in the bible do not relate to us today, but the theological message does. We need to take that message, the real meaning of the text and apply it to our audience in a way that demands action.

All of this sounds like hard work, and of course, it is! We are handling the word of God and therefore we need to take it seriously and invest whatever effort is necessary to make it understandable to those to whom we preach. However, like any skill, the more you do it the more natural it becomes. The very best of preachers are the ones who automatically do this work as they read the Bible because developing a good understanding of the text has become second nature to them.

CHAPTER 5

Dealing with biblical genre:
The Old Testament

Stephen McQuoid

One of the things I have enjoyed doing is to read bedtime stories to my children. Sadly these days my children are well beyond this stage. Generally, I read them Bible stories but sometimes I read stories from Greek mythology, or factual histories, or even fairy tales. On one occasion I was reading a fairy tale to my son called *The Story of the Nail Soup* which is one of the stories I have read to all my children at different times. At the half way point in the story my son interrupted and said, 'Is this a true story dad?'

I couldn't help but smile at his naiveté, however it did illustrate a very important point to both of us and that is you cannot read a fairy tale in the same way as you would read a factual history. The reason for this, of course, is that a history book is a different type of literature to a book of fairy tales.

When it comes to reading the Bible we need to realise that it is actually a collection of sixty-six books and that these are divided into different categories of literature. We refer to these categories as genres. There are several in both the Old and New Testaments and we need to know how each genre should be read if we are to make sense of it. Each genre will have particular rules that govern its use and if we apply these rules, we can grasp the meaning of the text.

Narrative

We begin in the Old Testament and start with the most common genre comprising almost half of the Old Testament: narrative. When we talk about narrative, we are referring to the stories of the Old Testament. These are true stories, actual historical accounts of what went on. Typical of stories in general, the stories of the Old Testament have a plot; they involve characters; and they have a setting. Of course, they are not ordinary stories because they form part of God's Word. They are stories with real theological meaning, not because they tell us what to believe or do, but rather because they show us what to believe or do. We learn by observing what goes on in the story and from this we can extrapolate theological meaning.

People enjoy stories and when it comes to the stories of the Old Testament, they too are enjoyable. They depict real life in all its colour and are vivid and compelling. We see real characters in real situations, and we can often identify with them and their situations. However, the real meaning, the lessons that God is trying to teach us, can often be subtle and so we need to read carefully and think clearly if we are to really benefit from these stories.

Narrative: plot

We begin reading narrative by paying close attention to the plot. It is the plot that makes the narrative work by giving us a sequence of events that show what the characters are doing and how this affects them and others. Sometimes a bigger plot can be composed of several smaller ones joined together. Take the life of David for example. We have the bigger plot of his life: his rise and then subsequent fall. However, within the overall plot of the life of David there are several smaller ones. These include his battle with Goliath (1 Samuel 17) or his friendship with Jonathan (1 Samuel 18-20) or even his sparing of Saul's life (1 Samuel 24). When you identify the plot, you need to ask what is going on, what events are being mentioned and how does it conclude? You also need to ask if there are any conflicts or other issues taking place. Each of these should be carefully noted as within them is the real meaning of the narrative.

Narrative: setting

Next you need to think about the setting. Think of the setting as the stage upon which a play is enacted. The setting tells you where the events took place and when. If you were watching a play in a theatre you would look at how the stage is set out which gives you clues as to the setting. You would also look to see if the actors are playing a scene during the day or the night time and their costumes would tell you is it is a modern day play or something that happened years ago.

Much the same is true of the biblical settings within a narrative. Are the events being described taking place in a palace, a field, up on a mountain or in a house? Is it daylight, early in the morning or midnight? It is important also to note whether the setting changes. For example, in Exodus 2 the setting at the start of the chapter is a riverbank, then it changes to the palace and by the middle of the chapter the setting is the wilderness of Midian, only to return to the slave camps of Egypt by the end of the chapter. These different settings speak volumes about what is really going on in the narrative.

Narrative: characters

Thirdly you need to think about the characters in the narrative. What kind of people are they, how do they behave, what is their attitude to God and to other people? Are they good, kind, honest or are they cruel, wicked and deceitful? The character of the characters is the most important thing of all. This is because we will learn theological lessons from observing what happens to people who behave in a particular way. For example, in 2 Samuel 11 while David's men go and risk their lives defending his kingdom, he is lying in his bed and then sleeping with the wife of one of his soldiers. This is also a good example of the contrasting characters that appear in narratives because Uriah remains a man of honour, faithfulness and integrity throughout—the complete opposite of the king he is serving.

Narrative: perspective of the narrator

A final thing to look out for is the perspective of the person who is telling the story, the narrator. It is not always easy to find out what his perspective is, but look hard and you will probably find it. Clues are to be found in the comments he makes which interpret that narrative. Perhaps the most notable of these can be found in the very last verse of the book of Judges where the narrator tells us that 'In those days Israel had no king; everyone did as they saw fit' (Judg. 21: 25).

Once you have observed all these features of narrative you are able to read it competently. You will be able to observe what kind of people were in the story because their actions reveal who they really are. You can see the actions within the plot and the setting. You can observe how God dealt with the characters. The narrator will also sometimes help you. When all of this is brought together, lessons can be learned.

Poetry

A very different genre within the Old Testament is that of poetry. Some of the books of the Old Testament are entirely poetry, such as the *Psalms, Song of Solomon, Proverbs* and *Lamentations*. Others, such as *Job, Ecclesiastes, Isaiah, Hosea* and *Joel*, contain substantial sections of poetry. Poetry is a recognisable art form in many cultures but again we need to remember this is the word of God so this is a unique kind of poetry that has real spiritual meaning. If you were to read a poem in English most probably rhyme would be a key feature. However Hebrew poetry is very different as it depends on a device called parallelism. This is a device that develops an idea by repeating it in different ways in succeeding lines. When you see this happening, it is a sure sign that you need to look carefully at what is being said and how it is being expressed.

The most common type is called *synonymous parallelism*. This is the repetition of the same thought using closely related but slightly differing sets of words. Psalm 103: 10 is a good example:

> He does not treat us as our sins deserve
> or repay us according to our iniquities.

Another type is *antithetic parallelism*. This is when the same idea is expressed in a different way in the second line by using words that are opposite of the first words. By using an opposite set of words, the writer can emphasize his point by making a contrast. An example of this type of parallelism is found in Psalm 37:21:

> The wicked borrow and do not repay,
> but the righteous give generously;

A third type is a *climactic parallelism*. Here the lines are repeated in such a way that they bring the reader to a crescendo. Climactic parallelisms usually have several lines and if read properly, the reader will feel a growing sense of excitement with each line. An example can be found in Psalm 29: 1:

> Ascribe to the Lord, you heavenly beings,
> ascribe to the Lord glory and strength.
> Ascribe to the Lord the glory due to his name;
> worship the Lord in the splendour of his holiness.

Then there are *emblematic parallelisms* which use analogy to develop a thought. Something is compared to another thing from a completely different sphere of life, for example, God being compared to a rock. This analogy enables the reader to visualise what the poet is saying. An example of this can be found in Psalm 42:1:

> As the deer pants for streams of water,
> so my soul pants for you, my God.

Often difficult to identify, depending on the translation, are *pivot parallelisms* which use a phrase as a central pivot between two lines. An example of this can be seen in Psalm 98:2 with 'to the nations' being the pivotal phrase:

> The Lord has made his salvation known
> *to the nations*
> and revealed his righteousness

Lastly there is *chiasmus*. In this poetic device an idea is put forward and is followed by two more ideas which relate to each other. Then there is a fourth idea which relates to the first one. A well-known example of chiasmus is in the Hebrew of Psalm 1: 1:

> Blessed is the one who does not walk in step with the
> wicked…but whose delight is in the law of the Lord.

One of the best ways of demonstrating chiasmus is by using the letter X to give it structure[10]:

Walk	Wicked
Sinners	Stand

It is important when reading poetry to pick out the parallelisms as they are there to focus your attention on what is being said. Ask yourself how the poet has expressed himself in this parallelism and you will be very close to finding its meaning.

It is important when reading poetry to pick out the parallelisms as they are there to focus your attention on what is being said. Ask yourself how the poet has expressed himself in this parallelism and you will be very close to finding its meaning.

Imagery

As well as using parallelism, Hebrew poets also made use of imagery in the form of simile and metaphor. A simile is where two things are being compared to each other using the words 'like' or 'as'. I could describe my wife as being 'like a beautiful flower'. A metaphor, on the other hand, compares two things in a much more overt way. For example, I could say my wife *is* a beautiful flower. Metaphors and similes are very common in biblical poetry and are frequently used in relation to God. The psalmist, for example, describes God as a rock, a fortress and a good shepherd.

The most obvious poetry in the Old Testament is found in the book of Psalms where we discover different kinds of Psalms. Some Psalms are *hymns* in which people are enthusiastically called upon to worship God. Others are *laments* where people cry out to God in distress. Still others are *thanksgiving poems* or *poems of confidence* in which the writer is either expressing thanks to God for his goodness or recognising reasons why God can be trusted. There

---

10 For a more detailed explanation of this figure of speech, see also https://www.etsjets.org/files/JETS-PDFs/17/17-1/17-1-pp011-028_JETS.pdf

are also *remembrance poems* which recall God's goodness to Israel in the past and *wisdom poems* where different ways of living are contrasted, and the results described. Whatever the type of Psalm, take careful note of how it works because that helps you to unpack its meaning.

How do we really grasp poetry and understand it? Firstly, you need to think about the experience that lies behind the poem. Psalm 51 is an obvious example. This was written after David committed the sin of adultery with Bathsheba and then covered it up by having her husband killed. This psalm is profoundly moving, and it expresses the deep-seated guilt that brought David to a point of confession and repentance. Discovering the experience enables us to see why the psalm was written.

A second step would be to identify and structure within the poem. Even at a first glance it is possible to see that many biblical poems are made up of stanzas (self-complete units of sense which build the structure like paragraphs in prose). These help to break up the poem so that the reader can see where it is going. For example, in Psalm 1 the first half deals with the righteous and their blessings while the second half is all about the wicked and the consequences of their actions.

Thirdly it is good to identify any difficulty which the writer may be facing and then see how this difficulty is solved. In Psalm 3 David was surrounded by many enemies but he realised that God was his shield and would protect him no matter what the difficulty. Taking these simple steps opens up the meaning of the poetry.

Prophecy

Another important genre within the Old Testament is that of prophecy. Numerous books of the Old Testament fall into this category. Some are large, like the book of Isaiah, whereas others are short such as Nahum. It is important to see the big picture in prophetic literature. Throughout the latter history of Israel, God sent men to bring his word to the people when they had fallen away from their faith. These men lived in the same cultural context as their contemporaries and they spoke in a language that their audience could understand. Their messages were contemporary to their time, yet they spoke out direct revelations from God. Often people make the assumption that the prophets were speaking about the future and it is true to say that a great deal of prophetic literature is predictive. However much of it was also a commentary on what was happening at the time when the prophets were ministering.

It is important to grasp that there were different kinds of prophetic utterances. For example, there were *prophecies of disaster*. These were delivered to individuals in some instances, to whole nations in others. Jeremiah 28:12—14 is one typical example. Linked with prophecies of disaster were *woe speeches*. These are easy to identify because they begin with the phrase 'woe to you'. A good example of a woe speech is in Amos 5:18—27 where the prophet pronounced judgment on the false spirituality of his time.

Some prophets also used a *funeral dirge*. These were usually directed towards Israel and she was pictured as a corpse awaiting burial (Amos 5:1—3). Perhaps the most interesting form of prophecy was the *prophetic lawsuit*. This kind of prophecy is best read with the imagination. The prophet re-enacts a court scene with Israel in the dock. Witnesses are called upon to give testimony against Israel and the nation is duly indicted as a result of the charges. Hosea 4:1—3 provides a typical example of this.

Not all prophecies are dour or have negative content. Some provided hope for the nation and called upon the people to return to God and to serve him faithfully. Some of these are described as *prophetic hymns*, for example Isaiah 42:10—13. Others we call *salvation prophecies* because the prophet assures both individuals and the nation that God would help them (Amos 9:11-15).

It is important to understand just how the predictive prophecies come to be fulfilled. In many cases there is a literal fulfilment in precisely the manner the prophet described. At other times, however, the prophecies were fulfilled figuratively. There were occasions when prophecies were fulfilled both literally and spiritually. In some cases, there have even been multiple fulfilments. Take for example Daniel's prophecy dealing with the abomination of desolation (Dan. 9: 27; 11: 31; 12: 11). It was first fulfilled when Antiochus Epiphanes made the Jews sacrifice pigs within the Holy of Holies in the Temple in 167 BC. It was then fulfilled again at the destruction of Jerusalem 70 AD and will be fulfilled a third time according to Mark 13:14.

Prophecy: historical setting

How do we come to understand the meaning of the prophets? Firstly, we need to discover the circumstances in which the prophet ministered. We do this by discovering how the people mentioned were living; in what ways they were falling short of God's standards; and any good or bad points that the prophet makes about them. This background information will enable us to see the relevance of the prophetic message for us today.

Prophecy: symbolism

We also need to pay close attention to the symbolism which the prophets use. In the same way that poetry is brought to life and made more descriptive through imagery, so prophetic literature is made more powerful by the use of symbolism. Jeremiah uses the symbol of a potter to demonstrate that God wants His people to be malleable and willing to be moulded by a divine hand (Jer. 18: 4). Amos uses the symbolism of a lion, a bear and a snake to demonstrate the inevitability of God's judgment (Amos 5:19). Ezekiel uses the symbolism of eating books to show that he was bringing God's message to the people (Ezek. 3:1-3).

It is also important to pick up on the reasons for judgment as this will also be included in the text. In Haggai the people were being judged because they were living in comfort while the Temple was in ruins (Haggai 1: 4). In Habakkuk judgment was imminent because the people were living unholy lives (Hab.1: 3-4). As we amass all of this information, we begin to see the message that lies behind the prophets' words and the meaning becomes clear.

Wisdom

One final genre that we need to think about is wisdom. No other genre within the Old Testament is as fascinating as wisdom literature and it is a very distinct genre. It does not contain the decisive voice of prophecy or the kind of blunt commands you would find in a passage such as Exodus 20. Rather the wisdom books are the thoughtful comments of teachers who are reflecting on the complexities of life.

There are four wisdom books: Proverbs, Job, Ecclesiastes and Song of Songs and each has its distinctive tone and message. Wisdom literature is often difficult to interpret because it deals with very deep and philosophical subject matter and does so by generalising and often leaving questions unanswered. What is more there is no equivalent genre in English. We therefore need to take care as we read and bear in mind that we will not always get neatly packaged answers from these books. They fully recognise that life is too complex for that. However, the benefits are enormous as these books provide us with a practical guide for living.

Wisdom literature is mainly poetic and so will contain parallelism and imagery. As we approach the wisdom books, we need to realise that whereas the other Old Testament books call upon us to obey, wisdom books call us to think hard.

Proverbs

The key verse in Wisdom literature is Proverbs 1:7, *The fear of the Lord is the beginning of knowledge.* Wisdom books provide a practical theology for everyday living. It would also be important to note that each wisdom book makes a distinctive contribution to our understanding. The book of Proverbs presents us with a rational way of living an ordered life. Its common sense approach deals with everyday themes such as friendship, marriage, speech, money and integrity. Many Proverbs are not universal in the sense that they are not always true in every circumstance but they do refer to what is generally true in normal life. For example when Proverbs 22:6 says, *Start children off on the way they should go, and even when they are old they will not turn from it.* This is not a guarantee that this will work in every family. It is generally true but there will always be exceptions. We need to think through these lessons and apply them to the whole of our lives.

Job

The book of Job, on the other hand, asks the huge question, why do the innocent suffer? Job reminds us that there are events in life which we simply cannot grasp or understand. Tragedy strikes and God does not disclose the reasons for this. It reminds us that God cannot be domesticated. We cannot expect him to protect us from all harm or answer all of our questions. It deals with real world experience and helps us to understand that we can still trust him when the world seems to be disintegrating all around us.

The big lesson from the book of Job is that often there are no simple answers and if we deal with suffering in a superficial way we will get it wrong. God is sovereign and we should never assume he no longer loves us or that he has lost control but rather we need to have faith in a time of crisis.

Ecclesiastes

Ecclesiastes is very different again as the writer is on a search for meaning. He is a wise man who enjoys all the privileges of life but ultimately finds them to be unsatisfying. The true meaning of the book is found in the closing verses where we read that true meaning can only be found in a good relationship with God. Logic and wisdom can help us day to day but only God can give ultimate meaning.

Song of Songs

Song of Songs is perhaps the most misunderstood of the wisdom books. Some have incorrectly read it as a picture of our relationship with Christ. This extreme allegorising is wide of the mark. These songs celebrate sexual love and the emotions that accompany a relationship between a man and a woman. It is written not so much to help us think logically about relationships but rather to help us celebrate God's good gift of companionship and sexual intimacy.

Whatever the wisdom book, remember the writer is not giving us simple answers to problems or trying to lay down rules for living. Instead he wants us to think about life in all its complexity and colour and to learn to live wisely. This pathway to a life well-lived begins with us having a profound respect for God and a submission to his will in our lives.

CHAPTER 6

Dealing with biblical genre:
The New Testament

Stephen McQuoid

'I don't preach much from the Old Testament' a friend of mine told me. 'I stick to the New Testament because it's so much easier to understand'. This is probably a fairly commonly held view among many preachers. They think that the Old Testament is hard work with its complex genre and detailed histories. Certainly it is true that the Old Testament presents the preacher with a great challenge but that does not mean that the New Testament is easy. It may be more familiar to most Christians and of course it is shorter than the Old but the New Testament still contains a number of genre which need to be thought about carefully before they can be mastered.

Gospels

The first of these that we need to think about are the gospels which at first glance appear to be no more than just narratives. However they are not as simple as that, because their unique subject matter, complex literary forms and theological emphases, mean that they merit a category of their own.

Within the gospels there is a division because Matthew. Mark and Luke share a great deal of material and so are often referred to as the synoptic gospels (synoptic meaning 'seen together'). John on the other hand has his own distinctive content and style.

There is a sense in which the gospels could be described as biographies of Jesus but this description doesn't quite fit because they are incomplete. Neither John nor Mark mention the birth of Christ while the order of events in the life of Christ differ according to which gospel you read. It becomes clear that each gospel writer has a particular perspective and he utilizes the stories of Jesus in order to get that point across. Despite this, the gospels are biographical as they do tell the story of Jesus. We could describe them as theological biographies, not just giving us facts but telling us who Jesus really is. We should also realize that ancient biographies apply rules which are different from those applied to modern ones. They generally begin with the birth of the character, devote a lot of space to the character's death and then arrange the material in a way that made a particular point about the character. This is exactly how the gospels work.

As you read through the gospels you will notice that the sequence of events varies depending on which gospel you are reading. This is because the gospel writers are not trying to be strictly chronological. They also feel free to paraphrase and summarize so any apparent discrepancies between the gospels should not concern us. They have a target audience in mind which also influences how they tell the story of Jesus. Mathew, for example, is writing for a Jewish audience hence the lengthy genealogy at the beginning which will appeal to them. Luke is writing for a nobleman called Theophilus which explains his attention to detail. Mark was written at a time when Nero was persecuting the Christians and so he reminds them that Jesus was the suffering servant. John tells us his purpose in 20:31, namely that through reading his gospel people will know Jesus is the Son of God and believe in him.

How are we to understand the gospels? The first thing we need to do is to grasp their general historical context. We come across groups like the Pharisees and the Sadducees; or people like King Herod and Pilate the Roman governor. We are introduced to tax collectors, freedom fighters and a political situation that is clearly volatile. All of these, as well as numerous mentions of local customs, are pieces of information that we need to know about if we are really to make sense of the gospels.

We should also have the gospel writer's motivation in the back of our minds as we read so that we view the stories of Jesus as he does. In addition we need to look for the key theme which weaves itself throughout the gospels, namely the Kingdom of God. Most Jews in Jesus day believed they lived on the very brink of a time when God would step into human history and usher in a new and better age. This messianic age would be a time when God would establish his rule and there would be peace and righteousness throughout the land (Isa. 2: 2-4; 11: 4-5). Jesus declared that the kingdom of heaven was near (Mark 1:14—15; Matt. 3: 2) but his picture of the kingdom was different to the one held by the Jewish religious authorities. If you can unpick why, then you begin to understand the gospels. It also makes sense of the miracles and the exorcisms of Jesus because he proved who he was by what he did (Lk.11: 20). After his resurrection there were those who wondered if he would usher in the kingdom (Acts 1: 6). This did not happen but he did send the Holy Spirit to help Christians live out kingdom values in their own lives. The ministry of Christ was therefore not the end of the age, but it was the beginning of the end. The final end will come with his second coming but in the meantime we live as kingdom people under the rule and authority of Christ.

Parables

All of this brings us to the parables which, while embedded within the gospels, are nevertheless a category all of their own. As we read the parables we should interpret them as narrative fiction. In other words, they are short stories that communicate meaning when studying the perspective of the main characters. They also frequently contain allegory, such as the parable of the sower where the sower is an allegorical figure who stands for Christ.

When we look at the parable of the Lost Son we see how the characters in the story lead us to the meaning (Lk. 15: 11-32). Each of the characters has something important to communicate. The lost son teaches us that the best way forward in a situation where rebellion has led to trouble and heartache is to repent. The father in the story teaches us something about the love of God while the older brother tells us something about a begrudging attitude towards God's blessing of others.

If we can view the gospel material as the authors did, and understand the historical background, this will help us to understand what each passage has to teach us. When it comes to the parables we need to understand how and why

Jesus told these stories and see what each character has to teach us and also note what, if anything, each component in the parable is meant to represent. Do all this and the gospels will become clearer and more meaningful.

Acts

After the gospels we have the book of Acts which is a single account of the story of the early church told by Luke. He utilises the same style as in his gospel with a carefully researched account of the key events in the history of the early church. Like the gospels, the book of Acts is a narrative. In the same way as the gospels are theological biographies, the book of Acts is theological history because the events in the book are presented in a way that reveals much about God's purpose in the world through the church. We are to learn lessons about church life today by what we learn about the conduct of the church then.

There are various key themes that can be identified in Acts. There is the theme of God's sovereignty as the church survives and then grows against all odds. Then there is the spread of the gospel from Jerusalem through to Judea and then to the rest of the world (Acts 1: 8) and going from within Judaism to reaching the gentile world. There is the theme of suffering as Stephen, Peter, Paul and the whole body of believers are hounded by Jewish leaders, pagans and Romans alike. Finally there is the theme of the promised Holy Spirit who comes upon the disciples in the upper room (Acts 2) and empowers them for mission.

Included in this portrait is the idea of a specific call into mission (Acts 13: 2). One of the key interpretive issues in the book of Acts is whether it is descriptive or normative. In other words, is the book a description of what did happen in the early church or is it a picture of what should always happen in church life everywhere? This question is particularly important when looking at the passages that deal with the Holy Spirit because if Acts is normative then we should expect to see the events of Acts 2 manifesting themselves in churches today. We would also be required to pool all our resources and expect God to judge people as he did with Ananias and Sapphira.

The best way of interpreting Acts is to see it as both. Some situations we should expect to see repeated today whereas others were particular to the events and times mentioned in Acts. The best way of distinguishing between the two is to look for the major movements in the book. Acts is significant theologically because the gospel spreads across some of the great barriers of the ancient world. Initially the Christians are Jews and they alone are blessed with the gift of the Spirit. Then in Acts 8 the Spirit comes upon Samaritan believers and the church ceases to be exclusively Jewish. Then in Acts 10 the Spirit comes on gentile Christians and the gospel is offered to the whole world. These are seismic events and they are accompanied by particular happenings that are associated with this theological development but which we should not expect today.

If we get this balance we will interpret Acts successfully.

Epistles

From the gospels and Acts, we turn to the epistles — twenty-one in total, which are letters written to individuals, churches or groups of churches. The epistles are arguably the most theologically compact texts in the whole of Scripture and follow a general literary pattern of five main parts:

    a. Opening greeting
    b. Thanksgiving (for the memory and well-being of the recipients)
    c. Main content of the letter
    d. Moral exhortations
    e. Closing comments

Often we make the mistake of just taking one verse in the epistles and using it in isolation. However they were intended to be read as a whole and so grasping the thought flow or logic of the argument is crucial to its understanding. We can also make the mistake of assuming that these letters were written to us. They were not! Herein lies one of the interpretive challenges of the epistles. A personal story will illustrate this.

Many years ago when I was a student I shared a house with five other students. The house was very small and had only two bedrooms, so every corner of the house seemed to have a bed in it. Living in such crowded conditions was often very annoying and as we all had different times for going to bed and very different lifestyles, it often felt like I would spend the whole three years of my degree without getting any sleep.

My mother used to write to me hoping to maintain contact and her letters always came enclosed in a distinctive white envelope. One morning after a long night of study, a letter arrived which I opened and began to read. I was puzzled because names were mentioned in the letter that I didn't know; situations were described that I had never heard of before; there was a question that didn't make any sense; and the letter stated that I had just been accepted for a job which I knew I hadn't applied for. Confused, I skipped to the very end of the letter only to see the words 'love Lillian'. I now knew that there had been a mistake because my mother was called Valerie. One of my housemates, on the other hand, was engaged to a girl called Lillian.

The reason for my confusion immediately dawned on me. It was not that the writer did not communicate clearly. On the contrary Lilian wrote beautifully. However I was not the person for whom the letter was intended so much of the content was a mystery to me.

Epistles: historical setting

Herein lies the challenge of understanding the epistles. We can only make sense of their content if we know something of the background. We can only know the background if we study more widely and also if we read the content very carefully looking for clues.

Epistles: authors

We begin by thinking about the author himself. What was his background? What was his relationship with the church or individual and why was he writing? Then we think about the recipients. Who were they and what were they doing? When these questions are answered we can begin to make sense of the content of the letters.

Often the writer will say both positive and negative things about the church. Essentially it was because some epistles, Paul's in particular, were follow-up letters to encourage fairly new churches some of which had lots of problems. For example when Paul wrote to the Corinthians he told them to 'stop thinking like children' about the way they used the gifts of the Holy Spirit (1 Cor. 14:20). He also warned the Thessalonians not to be lazy and hang about doing nothing while they waited for the second coming of Christ (2 Thess. 3: 6—10). In Ephesians 6 Paul tells the Christians in Ephesus to put on the armour of God because he knew what tremendous spiritual oppression they faced living in their multicultural city. Then in Galatians 5: 22-23 he urges the Christians there to live out the fruit of the Spirit which was the best response to the dead legalism of the Judaizers.

Epistles: reading the details

As well as getting the 'big picture' when it comes to the epistles we also need to notice the little details. Take note of the verbs and tenses which the writer employs. There are many instances where identifying the correct tense of a verb will have a profound effect on how we read a verse. In Ephesians 5:18, for example, Paul tells the Christians in Ephesus to be 'filled with the Spirit'. In this instance Paul is not referring to a one-off event, rather the verb is in the present continuous tense and so means something more like 'Keep being filled with the Spirit'. Also look at how the writer has chosen to structure his letter. Generally speaking Paul covers key theological issues first before having some practical application. He also sometimes diverts to cover a completely different subject as he did in Romans 9-11 where he includes a lengthy section on his own sorrow that so many Jews had not recognised the Messiah.

If you approach all of the epistles in this way, carefully reading the authors' comments and trying to imagine the situation that prompted the writing, then they open up and begin to make sense.

Apocalyptic

One final form of New Testament genre that we need to think about is apocalyptic. There are strands of apocalyptic writing in the Old Testament and when we come to the book of Revelation, the whole thing with the exception of the first three chapters is apocalyptic. This form of literature incorporates vivid and unusual pictures with symbolic meanings to communicate its message.

Apocalyptic literature deals with the end of world history and it comes to the writer in the form of visions and dreams. The subject matter often includes God's answer to the dilemmas of the world, which man has been utterly unable to solve. The symbolism is imaginative and even bizarre and it depicts future as well as present events. The big danger is to assume that apocalyptic will give a clear and specific timescale for the future. It was not written to do so. Rather its intention is to demonstrate the reality of the battle of good over evil and deliver the assurance that good will triumph.

As you read apocalyptic it is important to discover whether the symbolism in the passage would have had any significance to the writer in his culture. In Revelation 12:9. for example, the passage clearly states that the dragon is the devil and in Revelation 5: 8 we are told that the bowls of incense are the prayers of the saints.

Take care also when dealing with some of the numbers in apocalyptic literature as they are also sometimes symbolic. In Revelation we are told about a period of 1260 days or forty two months (Rev. 13: 5) and about the 144,000 (Rev. 14: 1). We also read about the great age of 1,000 years, known as the millennium (Rev. 20: 4) and the army of 200,000,000 men (Rev. 9: 16). Certainly these numbers mean something but they are not necessarily meant to be taken literally.

These then are the genre of the New Testament. They can be hard work to master, but hugely rewarding as they demonstrate the fulfilment of God's plan of redemption and enable us to understand the Godhead, the saving work of Christ and our responsibility as Christians to live for his glory.

The Bible as a whole is a massive work. God has spoken and has done so over the centuries. This magnificent book is the product of his voice. We need to treasure it and work hard to unpack its depths. We should never impose our own meaning in the word of God but rather allow it to speak for itself. We should also see it as a unified work and never build a doctrine from an illustration or an ambiguous verse taken out of context. Always ask what the author intended to communicate and recognise that revelation is progressive and that the earliest books of the bible will not contain a fully-orbed revelation of God or his purposes. Differentiate between what is said about Israel and what is said about the church. Acknowledge that we are sinful and therefore cannot fully comprehend God's revelation and have the humility to listen to the opinions of mature Christians who will help you to understand more fully. These qualities are the mark of a good interpreter and preacher.

CHAPTER 7

Erecting the Scaffolding:
Producing a sermon outline

Jeremy McQuoid

It is always a fateful moment when the preacher says, 'and thirdly…' and you cannot remember points one and two! The problem is sometimes down to your memory, but more often than not, it is because the preacher has not planned out his message carefully enough. The reason why so many sermons lack clarity is that no clear sermon outline has been thought through. A sermon that is coherent – introducing, developing and driving home the 'big idea' of the text you are preaching – needs a good sermon outline.

Before you can preach an effective sermon that everyone understands, you need to erect the scaffolding – put together an outline or skeleton of your big idea and main points, and have some idea of the conclusion you are aiming for, before you ever start writing your sermon. In my preaching classes at Gordon Conwell Seminary in Boston, Dr. Haddon Robinson used to say, 'a mist in the pulpit is a fog in the pew'. If the preacher does not know where he is going with his sermon, what chance do his listeners have!

I usually spend about 5 mornings a week putting together a sermon, and only 2 of those mornings are spent writing up the manuscript. Three full mornings are spent studying the text, finding the big idea and main points of the text, and then translating that into a sermon outline. I find I can write my manuscript much more quickly, and develop an excitement about what I am going to preach, when I have spent significant time constructing the outline. If I rush that process because I feel pressurized to produce a sermon, I will come unstuck later on (and the listeners will start looking at their watches early!). This chapter outlines the process I go through to produce a sermon outline.

Begin with examining the text closely

Begin with immersing yourself in the text you are preaching, until you understand what it is saying, and how it is saying it. At this stage you are not thinking about how to apply the text (though some ideas might come to mind that you can jot down). You are simply tracing the flow of thought in the passage, and grappling with what the writer is saying.

It is good to read a text 3 or 4 times, using different translations, so that you capture the flow of thought. I would note down the main ideas of the passage on a piece of paper, and keep reading and adjusting those main ideas, until I have a firm grasp of what the passage is saying.

If I have questions in my mind about the text, I will note them down, and look perhaps for a commentary to answer them eventually. But it is important that you do not rush to commentaries too quickly. Commentaries can provoke thought and stir ideas, but they cannot give you a sermon. It is important that you 'own' your sermon. You cannot communicate passionately what you have borrowed from someone else, so you need to let the Word impact your own soul, until you make your own discoveries, and develop your own convictions from the text.

Reading the Commentaries

When you have gone as far as you can in noting down the flow of thought in the passage, and jotting down some ideas of what application might begin to look like, then you can turn to commentaries. But be careful! Many commentaries are written for academics, not for preachers, and seem intent on telling you everything about the passage apart from what it means! (We note in Appendix C the kind of commentaries we have found helpful).

Don't read a very lengthy, technical commentary to begin with. Find a practical commentary (the *Tyndale* commentaries and *Bible Speaks Today* series are excellent in this regard) whose main aim is to tell you what the passage means in practical terms, without skimping on scholarship. Then you can skim through a more technical commentary to see if it makes any interesting points about verbs or tenses, or something you won't find out anywhere else.

To finish your commentary reading, try and find a commentary that is written from a preacher's point of view. Sadly there are few of these around, but I have found Kent Hughes' *Preach the Word* series and Warren Wiersbe's 'Be' series helpful, along with the *NIV Application* series. You might not agree with some of the applications these preachers' commentaries give, but it is helpful to start thinking 'how might these points look in a sermon,' and you can start to make the transition in your mind between an accurate understanding of the text (exegesis), and the kind of sermon your exegesis might lead to (homiletics). Your job as a preacher is not simply to tell your listeners what the text means, but to apply that text to the lives of your hearers and move their hearts to want to obey.

Finding the 'big idea'

By now you should have read and thought a lot about the meaning and application of the passage, so it is time to construct a brief outline, which begins with finding the big idea. Put together a compact, hopefully 'catchy' sentence or phrase that summarizes the main theme of the passage. This sentence is not simply reproducing what the text is saying, but moving towards 'mustness'. What *must* I do in response to this passage? What is the 'take home truth' for my life in this passage?

The average listener is waiting for application to daily life, so don't spend so much time in explaining the text, that application simply comes at the end when your listener has already 'zoned out'. Prof. Don Carson, my former lecturer at Trinity Evangelical Divinity School, used to say in our exegesis classes that 50% of your whole sermon time should be spent developing application, and Dr. Grant Osbourne emphasized the need to find application as early as possible in a sermon so that people don't lose interest.

If your big idea is 'Jesus is the light of the world', that is simply restating what the text says. A better big idea would be 'Because Jesus is the light of the world, we need to obey his Word.' A big idea needs to tell me, in a succinct phrase, how I should respond to the word of God today.

64 Learning to Preach

The best big ideas are almost like a slogan. I remember preaching at the funeral of a Christian lady in her thirties who had died tragically of cancer. I needed to help the congregation understand what God could have possibly been doing, allowing such a tragedy to occur.

I had visited this lady several times before she died, and noticed how much her faith grew through her cancer ordeal. And my 10 minute sermon at the funeral had the big idea 'God's goal in our lives is not to make us happy or successful, but to make us like Jesus.' And I kept on repeating that big idea throughout the message. It reflected what the Bible taught, but it was also a slogan that was easy to remember, and gave a clear understanding of how to respond to this tragic event.

Your main points must support your big idea

One of the most common errors among preachers is to make points about the text that are not connected to each other in any way. The points made may be true enough, and may arise from the passage, but if they do not derive from a single big idea, then the sermon becomes disjointed and hard to remember.

Studies have shown that the human mind retains best a single idea that is developed in various ways throughout a talk. Newspaper columnists follow through one coherent big idea in their articles. They raise an issue in their opening paragraphs that they then discuss in the body of their articles, and then form a conclusion which re-emphasizes and drives home the big idea. The message of the article is like an arrow, driving home one main point, rather than a 'scatter gun' approach that raises lots of disconnected issues.

Consider a sermon outline that looks like this:

Point 1 – some thoughts about self control
Point 2 – beware of false teachers
Point 3 – Jesus is coming again

Each of these points are biblical truths that may well have emerged from the passage, but they lack any sense of unity or progress. Compare that to the following outline

We should give our lives to Jesus because:

Point 1 – He created us

Point 2 – He died for us

Point 3 – He is coming again for us

The second outline would lead to a sermon that is coherent and easy to remember, where each point is tightly connected to the whole, and derives from the big idea.

Main points should parallel each other

Coherence comes not just from each main point deriving from one overall big idea that dominates the sermon, but ideally the main points should mirror each other. Note, each main point in the outline above begins with 'He', and ends with 'us', and each point contains a verb of something else Jesus does for us – he 'created' us, 'died for' us and is 'coming again' for us. And each of these points are 'reasons why we should give our lives to Jesus.' They all derive from, and point back to, the big idea.

Hearing a sermon like that would bring a satisfying sense of order, unity and progress. It would be easy to remember, and satisfying to listen to. You can usually tell when an outline has been well prepared, because you do not find yourself struggling to understand the structure of the talk as a listener. The structure is so clear that you spend your time thinking about the truth that is being delivered. However, when an outline is incoherent, you spend so much time trying to understand where the preacher is going, that you cannot take in what he is saying at any given point.

The first outline above is very difficult to remember. To begin with, the preacher would talk about 'self control' and then move on to talking about false teachers, without giving you any reason why he has moved from one point to another. He may say some perfectly good things about each topic, but it would be difficult to follow, and with the best will in the world, you cannot stop your mind trying to make connections between each point (that is how our brain has been created to work) that simply aren't there. Such a sermon would also lead you to the conclusion that the Bible itself is an incoherent jumble of moral commands, when it is so much more coherent and sophisticated than that.

Writing up the Manuscript

After you have produced an outline that is coherent, it is time to write out your manuscript, word for word. Many young preachers protest at this point that this is too much work and unnecessary. 'Why can't I just put together of set of bullet points that follow the general drift of my sermon?'

It sounds reasonable, but we have found again and again that preachers who have not produced a full manuscript begin to waffle, drift, and lack precision. Some even slip into unintended heresy, or say something deeply inappropriate because they haven't thought carefully about each word, and create ideas 'on the hoof', which is so dangerous when eternal truth is at stake.

Writing a manuscript is exacting, and that is why it is so necessary. You can see the whole flow of your sermon, and think through clear transitions between your points. It's also easy to preach a full manuscript again elsewhere, but much harder to remember what you were meaning by each bullet point! Martin Lloyd Jones quipped that a sermon is not really ready until it has been preached at least four times! He gives us plenty of excuse to repeat well-crafted sermons in different settings, thoughtfully 'edited' for each new audience.

Transitions

Working out clear transitions between your main points is one of the least heralded but most important parts of clear preaching. Public speaking demands a lot more unsubtle transition than writing a book. When you read a book, you have transition markers like paragraph divisions and sub headings. You can also pause and re-read paragraphs if you lose the flow.

You do not have that luxury in public speaking. Speaking passes so quickly, and you only get one opportunity to hear and take it in, so you must make your transitions super clear, largely through summation and repetition. As one of my preaching professors said, 'You must tell people where you are going, repeat where you are going regularly, go there, and then tell them you have gone there!'

Here is an example of a good transition, using the outline above. We have just completed our first point 'we must give our lives to Jesus because he created us'. As I reach the hopefully rousing conclusion of my first point, I need to sum it up briefly and introduce my second point. The transitional statement may look something like this:

> So Paul is teaching us here that we need to give our lives to Jesus, and the first reason we should give our lives to Jesus is because he created us. But not only did he create us, secondly, he died for us. That's the second reason Paul gives us for why we should give our lives to Jesus – not just because he created us, but also because he died for us. Look at verses 4-6…

Notice the amount of repetition here, that would be overkill if this was a book, but vital because it is the spoken word. We repeat the big idea (we need to give our lives to Jesus) 3 times, we repeat the first point (because he created us) 3 times, and we introduce the second point (because he died for us) by repeating it twice.

If you had a transitional sentence like that, people would instantly realize that you are making a major transition in your sermon, and they would be clear how that transition is still connected to your overall big idea. What appears repetitive and redundant on paper brings clarity and purpose to those who are listening and only have 'one shot' at getting it right.

You need to be particularly unsubtle when transitioning, because you are so aware of where you are going in your own mind, you can easily under estimate how difficult it is for people to follow you, who have not been immersed in your passage all week! They have just a few moments to grasp changes of thought that you have been wrestling with and praying over for a week!

Ask someone else to read your completed manuscript

That's why we would encourage you to ask a close friend to read your manuscript before you preach. I usually hand my completed manuscript to my wife on a Friday before the Sunday I preach. I am nervous about that moment because it is the first time someone else is seeing my sermon creation that I have poured my heart into all week, and I rarely have an idea at that stage, if the sermon is clear, coherent or even interesting in the slightest! This process makes me feel vulnerable, and defensive, but I need to be open to critique before I launch my sermon on the world! I may love what I have written, but that counts for little if others don't share my enthusiasm!

I intentionally give my sermon to my wife for several reasons. Firstly she is close enough to me to tell me the unvarnished truth about the sermon. The more robust critique you can get of your sermon at this stage, the better for your hearers on Sunday. Get rid of the dross to leave the gold!

Secondly, she is a woman, and over half my audience are females, as is true of most churches in the West! Men like me can be blissfully unaware of how to preach to women, how women think, and what illustrations they relate to. If my sermon is filled with sports or military illustrations, I am likely to lose half my audience, so a female critique is especially helpful!

Thirdly, she can see things immediately that I cannot see because I have become too engrossed in my sermon – 'I can't see the wood for the trees!' There is no point me thinking the sermon is clear, if she cannot understand where I am going. I don't even get her to read the passage of scripture. I simply want her to tell me – 'is this coherent, does it make sense from start to finish? And if not, where did she get lost, and why?'

Fourthly, she helps me bring some 'finishing touches' that make all the difference. When we are having guests round for dinner, we use bright red paper serviettes that we stick into the glasses until they puff out in an artistic way. It only takes a few minutes to add the serviettes, but it makes a huge difference to the presentation of the meal!

In the same way my wife will often say of my sermon 'it's clear and biblical, but it needs an illustration here, or a quote there to lighten it up.' By 'lighten it up' she does not mean lighten the theology. She means 'you have spent so long explaining the point it risks becoming too dull or heavy. You need some contemporary illustration, or personal human story, to bring some relief and shine a new light on the point you are making.' I cannot count the number of times a truth filled but dull sermon has sparked into life because of an illustration my wife has 'driven' me to find. I didn't just marry her for her looks!

CHAPTER 8

Take-off and Landing:
Opening and closing a sermon well

Jeremy McQuoid

I was speaking to the editor of a well-known book publishing company recently. This person has a very influential role in the company because he decides on which manuscripts are chosen to publish and which manuscripts end up in the rubbish bin, never to see the light of day.

And he shocked me when he told me how he decides whether or not a manuscript is worthy of publication. This is not a word-for-word quote but he said essentially, 'I open the first chapter and if the theme of the book does not grab me on the first page, I'm not interested. I don't care how well the story develops, how interesting the plot twists are or how developed the characters are. In fact there are hundreds of manuscripts that I have never read beyond the first page. If I am not captivated by my first five minutes reading, I know it's for the scrap heap!'

The importance of a good introduction

Many preachers fail to grasp the importance of a sermon introduction. Whether you like it or not, every sermon has an introduction but we often stumble through it in an unsure manner waiting to get into the 'meat' of our text. But the sermon introduction is the time during the sermon when most people decide whether or not they are going to listen!

It doesn't matter if you have insightful points half way through your message or a brilliant illustration towards the end. If your listeners have already decided in the first five minutes that the sermon is not worth listening to, grabbing their attention in the middle of the sermon is almost impossible.

The aim of a sermon introduction is first and foremost to give our audience a reason to listen. We need to remember that our hearers have not spent the week absorbed in the fascinating passage we are studying. They have not read the commentaries and been drawn in to the argument.

Perhaps a fair number of them are not as gripped by the scriptures as you are. You have been called to be a preacher who spends his life studying and enjoying the scriptures. It doesn't take any imagination to get you interested in the Bible. But for most people who listen to our sermons, the Bible is not nearly as exciting as it is to us.

They need to be drawn in and given a good reason why they should spend the next thirty or forty minutes of their lives listening to your sermon. If you don't grab their attention in the first five minutes of your preaching, you are unlikely to keep them 'hooked' for forty minutes, especially in the 'sound bite' generation in which we live. So how can we draw them in?

Be clear about the 'big idea' of your message

The reason why many preachers struggle with introductions is because they have no clear idea what their sermon is about so they don't know how to introduce it! The aim of an expository sermon is not just to talk about various points that emerge from the passage but to present the challenge of the passage like an arrow to the human heart.

If your sermon revolves around disconnected points drawn at random from the text with no unifying theme or purpose for the sermon, then the arrow is blunted and it is almost impossible to know how to introduce the message.

Imagine the following sermon outline for a moment:

Point 1 – God calls us to be holy
Point 2 – A few thoughts about loving one another
Point 3 – The need for discipline in discipleship

Now each of these points may be drawn from the text and be full of truth but how would you introduce a sermon with those discordant, disconnected parts? Are you introducing the idea of being holy, or loving one another, or the need for discipline? If you are introducing the first point about holiness, your listener will then expect your whole sermon to be about holiness and so will sense discord when you suddenly move to point 2 about loving one another.

You may say some good things about loving one another but the mind of your listener will be confused about why, suddenly, you are talking about love when everything up to that point of the sermon had to do with holiness. After a while your listener will give up the fight to find coherence in your message because there is no coherence. That is not good communication.

A coherent message

Compare that to the following outline:

> Big idea: Be holy because…
> > Point 1 – God is holy
> > Point 2 – We are called to be holy like God
> > Point 3 – Ultimately we will be holy when we see Christ

It's not a perfect sermon outline but there is coherence running through it. The sermon has a definite single purpose. It is a call to *holiness* and each point builds from the previous and backs up the big idea so the listener will move seamlessly from one point to the next and feel intellectually satisfied when you 'drive home' your conclusion about holiness at the end of the message, because that has been your coherent theme all the way through.

And when you have a clear big idea like the one above, it makes the job of producing a clear introduction so much easier. I know exactly what my target is. The aim of my introduction would be to call my listeners to think about holiness, to entice them into holiness, to help them see that the next thirty minutes are going to be the most important thing in the world to listen to because it's all going to be a passionate call to holiness.

Start your introduction in this world

Not only do you need a coherent big idea and purpose for your sermon before you can form an introduction. You also need to start with a 'felt need' from today's world rather than launching straight into the biblical text. The aim of an introduction is to build a bridge between our lives today and the very different world of the text.

I once heard a preacher open his sermon with the words, 'Now today we find ourselves in Genesis 11, and we follow Abraham and his family as they make their move from Haran to Canaan'. If you heard that introduction, would you want to hear more? I wouldn't and most people today would not.

It makes me feel like I am about to listen to a dry Bible commentary about the passage rather than a message to stir my heart. The truth is most people sitting in front if you on a Sunday do not really care that Abraham went from Haran to Canaan or why he went. You have to tell them up front why this matters or else you will lose their interest.

Before I explain anything about the Bible passage, I want to convince my hearers that this passage is highly relevant to their lives today. The single mother with no Christian background sitting next to her special needs son on the fourth row could not care less why Abraham went from Haran to Canaan. She comes to church with huge struggles, barely able to cope with her own life and the only thing that is stopping her from baling out of life altogether is to hear a word from the Lord to keep her together, to give her some inspiring vision of God, to help her see why she is running this Christian race.

An 'Abraham-went-from-Haran-to-Canaan' introduction makes her feel that the Bible has nothing to say to her life when in reality it could change her whole understanding of life. But she will not listen unless she can tell right away that this message has something powerful to speak into her life situation.

Creative attention grabbing

Compare that sermon introduction to this one that I have stolen loosely from my preaching mentor, Dr Haddon Robinson. He preached this message in the unique setting of a woman's retreat. This is more or less how he introduced his sermon:

> I was walking in the [New York] subway and I saw this graffiti
> on the wall. Sometimes even graffiti can teach you more than
> you realise. And I noticed that this particular piece of graffiti
> was spelt wrong. The artist had written the word 'gril' rather
> than 'girl.' I wonder do you feel like a 'gril' sometimes, rather
> than a girl? Do you feel that life hasn't turned out the way you
> wanted? That none of your dreams and expectations of life
> have been met? You get an image of glamorous womanhood
> from the magazines, or the TV or the internet and every
> time it makes you feel like half a woman. You feel like a 'gril'
> and not a girl. If you feel like that, if you want to set aside
> the world's image of you and focus your heart on what God
> thinks of you, then come with me on a journey into the book
> of Ruth. God has a message for your life today. Open your
> Bible to Ruth chapter one.

My guess is that women on that retreat would be opening their Bibles to Ruth chapter one so quickly you could almost smell the pages burning. It is a good introduction because it feels immediately relevant. The setting is not Canaan 4000 years ago but New York today.

It is an intriguing introduction because you want to know where the preacher is going as he talks about graffiti that has been misspelt. And most of all it uncovers a felt need that all women everywhere have— what is my identity? What does it mean to be a woman today when glamour magazines are selling images that make me feel worthless and powerless? What does God have to say about this huge issue in my life?

Your attention is grabbed, the relevance is clear, the felt need is emotively raised and all within a couple of paragraphs and you are waiting and longing for what God has to say to you today.

Be Interesting

Haddon Robinson, probably the most influential teacher of preaching in the twentieth century, said, 'I have been closer to being bored out of Christianity than being argued out of it.' It takes more than just 'sound theology' to be a transformational preacher.

You need to be interesting. In a world advanced in media technology and sharp presentations, we cannot afford to be dull in the pulpit. And if we are not interesting in our introductions, it does not matter if we are interesting elsewhere in our message. When the prophets preached in Israel, they may have raised peoples' hackles but they certainly weren't dull. They were relevant, up-to-date, with penetrating insight.

Beginning a message in a contemporary setting, raising a felt need, perhaps using an illustration to draw your hearers in and keep them hooked, will inspire your listeners to want to hear more. You recognize the best preaching when people feel they just have to hear more.

Take more time to think about your introduction than you do about any other section of your message. Be creative, be direct, be relevant, raise a need that the Bible passage answers, and if you do, you will help your people see that the Scriptures are the answer to life's biggest questions, that they are far from dull and academic, they are alive with life-changing truth.

Landing the Plane

If introductions need special thought and preparation, then so do conclusions. I have heard many sermons where it is clear that the preacher does not know how to 'land the plane.' Anytime I fly down to the enormous Heathrow airport in London, I expect there to be a significant delay in landing. So many planes are trying to land at the same time that you can spend up to half an hour circling the airport before finally landing. It can be frustrating to be delayed when you know you are hovering over your final destination.

And that's how I feel when I listen to a preacher who does not know how to finish his sermon. You see him circling and circling without ever 'landing the plane'. It builds a sense of frustration. When is he ever going to finish? It is a cardinal rule of good preaching never to 'outstay your welcome' - that fateful moment when the congregation start rustling in their uncomfortable pews, stifling yawns, looking at their watches, wishing you would just sit down. How can we conclude in an inspiring way?

As we said for introductions, if you do not have a clear understanding of the big idea, the purpose of your sermon, it is difficult to know how to conclude it. Good conclusions mean driving home the main point that has been coherently presented throughout the sermon. If you do not have one coherent big idea and you end up trying to conclude a sermon based on several disconnected points, it is almost impossible to finish well.

How good your conclusion is depends greatly on how coherent your sermon has been — how focused on a single big idea. As we suggested above, that does not mean that you cannot have several different points in your sermon. But it is vital that each point serves and builds on the big idea before you drive that big idea home.

Again, imagine a sermon outline that looks something like this:

> Point 1 – Love one another
> Point 2 – Get ready for the return of Christ
> Point 3 – Keep your thoughts pure

All of these are valid points to make that might well have been drawn from the text, but how to do you conclude a sermon like that? It would be difficult to sum up all three points because they have no connection with each other and you will leave the listeners confused.

If you simply drive home your final point (keep your thoughts pure), then your listeners will not be able to remember your first two points and you will leave with the impression that the Scriptures are a series of proverbs or proof texts that lack coherence, a melange of disconnected commands when in reality every paragraph of Scripture has a deep unity and coherence.

Conclusions are only as good as your big idea

Compare that outline to the following:

> Big Idea: Get ready for Christ's return, because…
> > Point 1 – He's coming soon
> > Point 2 – He will come when no one is expecting
> > Point 3 – He will come to judge believers as well as non-believers

Again, each point serves and builds on the big idea of Christ coming again, so when you arrive at your conclusion, you know clearly the main point you want to drive home — 'Get ready for Jesus to return. Make this the highest priority of your life. Don't be living for this world. Pin your hope on the next!'

It's so much easier to force a point home that has been built up coherently, stage by stage, until it reaches a kind of crescendo at the end. You leave the congregation waiting and hoping for the crescendo rather than just longing for you to sit down!

Don't simply recap

If you listen to a great symphony, you will usually find that the symphony ends on a note of great triumph with the whole orchestra involved —making the hairs stand up on the back of your neck! Think of the 'Hallelujah Chorus' from Handel's *Messiah*.

It would have been a crying shame if the beauty of *The Messiah* finished with a whimper instead of a bang! Similarly many good sermons are destroyed when a preacher simply recaps what he has said without bringing a crescendo to his preaching.

I remember learning the word 'bathos' in school. Bathos is the idea of a 'come down', something that leaves you feeling flat like a football game with very exciting moments petering out to a dull draw. And simply recapping the points you have brought up in your sermon, no matter how good those points have been, inevitably leads to a sense of bathos. It leaves you, and your listeners, deflated at the very moment you most want to be uplifted.

Your highest point of emotion, your most passionate diction needs to be reserved for your conclusion. I have heard (and probably preached) several sermons where the high point is in the introduction or some moving moment in the middle but the conclusion is eminently forgettable. (Don't make your introduction so emotionally intense that the rest of the sermon is bound to be a 'come down'.) That concluding moment is such a vital time to make your hearers say 'I want to go and live this out now. I want to obey Christ. I want to worship.'

If they felt that way half way through the sermon but feel a sense of bathos at the end because you had simply recapped your sermon, they are less likely to put your sermon into practice than if they leave with spiritual momentum.

Finish with Focused Flourish

You need to finish your sermon with a flourish. But that does not mean finishing merely with flowery, poetic language. You need to finish with pointed real-life application as well. How can the truth I have raised in this sermon impact my life on a Monday morning? If I were finishing a message on the return of Christ, I would want to talk about the glory of that day but also relate it to tomorrow morning. Something like this…

> When you open your Bible to read tomorrow, do it with fresh enthusiasm because Christ is coming again. Go to work with a spring in your step because Christ is coming again. Witness with passion, increase your intensity in praying for those outside Christ, because Christ will burst through the clouds at any moment. Keep your thoughts holy. Keep your robes sparkling white because Jesus is coming again.'

In this conclusion there is a mixture of emotive, poetic language (keep your robes sparkling white, Christ will bust through the clouds) with clear, specific application. Do your daily Bible reading, witness to friends, work with enthusiasm.

Don't have a rhetorical flourish that isn't grounded in daily reality. And don't give practical examples without a height of emotion that a conclusion deserves. Put both together and 'finish with a focused flourish'. The last thing your listeners hear will be the first thing they think about afterwards.

Leave them with not just solid teaching, organized structure and faithful exposition. Leave them singing with the angels, moved to the core of their being with flaming hearts ready to serve the King of Kings!

CHAPTER 9

Windows on the world:
Illustrating your points

Stephen McQuoid

M ost of my preaching is done in my own church. I love preaching elsewhere, especially when it involves travel to other countries but there is nothing quite like preaching in your own church to people who know you well and who have heard you many times before. When I preach in my church I have the greatest asset that any preacher could have. — a family who are honest: a wife and three children who are supportive and encouraging and yet will tell me if I was hard to understand, or too long, or simply just boring. These honest critics are the greatest help I can have in my endeavour to become a better preacher.

When I get this feedback from my family, the most common complaint they have is that I often just explain what the passage says without really making it clearly understood. Many preachers are guilty of this and the solution is to use illustrations. An illustration is to a sermon what a window is to a house. If you were to build a house without windows, it would be very dark inside. With windows however, the whole house is full of light. In the same way illustrations illuminate what you are trying to say in your sermon.

Illustrations have several functions in a sermon. The first of these is that illustrations should bring understanding. The Bible is a wonderful book but it is not always easy to understand or communicate. There are many theological concepts in the Bible that are extremely difficult to grasp. How are we to understand the Trinity, or the doctrine of predestination? How do we express the wonder of the love of God, or of his eternal nature? Some of these concepts are so enormous, so elevated that the only way in which we can even attempt to understand them is by using an illustration.

This of course is something the Bible writers themselves did. The psalmist used the illustration of wild grass to demonstrate the mortality of human existence (Ps.103:15). The prophet Jeremiah used the illustration of a hammer smashing rocks to describe the impact of his message (Jer. 23: 29). Jesus also frequently used illustrations. for example in Matthew 5:13—14 he famously took the common objects of salt and light as an illustration of the impact his followers should have in the world. Later in 1 Thessalonians 2:7 Paul used the picture of a mother caring for her children to illustrate his commitment to the Christians in Thessalonica. A good illustration will help the listener really understand the point being made.

Secondly illustrations can help the preacher to retain the interest of his audience. This is actually a hugely important issue because no matter how good or theologically sound your sermon is, its value is limited if people are not really listening. It is not that we should preach to entertain but we should work hard at communicating in an absorbing way. Again Jesus himself did this. His parables are so memorable that they have become well-known stories in many countries. Preachers should work hard at holding people's attention and using illustrations is a very good way of doing this.

In general I try to have at least one illustration for every major point I am trying to make in a sermon. Often when I preach there are three or four major things I am trying to get across and the illustrations will keep people's attention and also make the points memorable.

One last thing we need to emphasize is that illustrations are also very good at motivating and enthusing our audience into action. When we get our points across to the audience we are not just giving them information rather we want them to respond with obedience and do what we are challenging them to do. This challenge can often best be communicated in the form of an illustration.

Some months ago I was preaching on the issue of humility from Philippians 2:3. Sometimes a subject like humility can appear very abstract and theoretical.

In order to avoid this I used an illustration. I told the story of a young missionary nurse who was working in a refugee camp in Congo. She was visited by a leader from her home church who wanted to see her at work. The small clinic she managed had run out of supplies so when a man came in with a large and badly infected wound, she had nothing to treat it with. Instead she had brought to the clinic some of her own clothes which she began to cut into strips. She used one strip to gently clean the filthy and foul-smelling wound. She then used a second strip to bandage the wound. Here the church leader, nauseated by the sight and smell of the wound, said to her, 'I would not do a job like that for a million dollars' to which she simply replied, 'Neither would I'.

I made the point that it was her love and humility that drove her to do that act of service, I could tell, just by looking at the faces of my audience that they had been inspired by the story and were ready to put what they had learned into practice.

Having pointed out the importance and value of illustrations, it is now time to sound a note of warning. This needs to be done because if we are not careful about how we use illustrations we are in danger of making some basic and needless mistakes. This is because while illustrations can greatly help your sermon they can also cause problems. So what problems do we need to avoid?

Illustrations that take over

Firstly we need to be careful that our illustrations don't take over when we are preaching. I have all too often made the mistake of using too many illustrations in my preaching and I am now self-consciously trying to be more self-controlled when I am preparing. This kind of a mistake usually happens when I have not done enough work in studying the text. In effect, I cover up my lack of knowledge of the text by using illustrations, firstly because they take up time and also because I know they are an easy way to hold peoples' attention. However if I do not properly communicate the full meaning of the text, then I am doing my audience a disservice. After all, my job is not just to tell interesting stories, it is to teach Scripture. The exposition of the text must be my primary goal and the illustrations serve that purpose.

Because of this particular danger I have come to the conclusion that there should be only one illustration for each point I make in my sermon and a sermon should never have more than six or seven illustrations. Don't allow the fear of losing your audience's attention force you into using more illustrations than is necessary. If you know your passage well, preach it with conviction, using illustrations wisely so that they are a help to understanding then people will listen and God can communicate through your spoken word.

Illustrations that draw the audience away

A second mistake to watch out for is using illustrations that take the audience's mind away from the points you are making in the sermon. This is a simple mistake to make and just as simple to correct. It is also obvious why this mistake happens. A preacher might use an illustration that does not really fit in with the point being made. Because of this the illustration actually causes confusion rather than assisting the listener to understand more clearly. Alternatively a preacher can rush through the point being made and then use an illustration that is so memorable that the listener remembers the illustration but has no recollection of the point being made in the first place.

I remember on one occasion preaching on the issue of sin and was making the point that the Bible describes us as prisoners to sin (Gal.3: 22). Rather than taking the necessary time to explain what Paul meant by this I went straight to an illustration which was a very gripping story. My hope was that this story would hit home the point with great force. Unfortunately I discovered later that most of the people who were listening to the message could remember the story I told but had no idea what the point of my message was. Again the illustration, while a good one, was counterproductive.

As I have already said, this kind of a mistake is quite easy to correct. Make sure that the illustration you use genuinely fits the point being made. If there is any possibility of confusion or ambiguity, don't use it. When you are using illustrations ensure that the point you are making is clearly explained and then use the illustration to support the point you have made. In this way make sure the illustration is the servant of the exposition and not the other way around.

Illustrations that are inappropriate

A third mistake is to use an illustration that is inappropriate to our audience. This kind of mistake happens most frequently when the preacher does not know much about his audience or has not taken the time to think about their situation and worldview. I once took one of my students to an old people's home to preach as I thought the experience would be good for him. He was only 18 years of age and so he needed to be exposed to a range of different ministry situations to compensate for his lack of experience of life. He actually preached very well and the elderly people who listened enjoyed what he had to say. However after making an important point in his sermon he used an illustration which centred on a famous dance music DJ and spoke as if his audience would know the person in question. I had to smile at his naivety as well as at the puzzled expressions of the old people who were totally lost at that point of the message. It was actually a very good illustration but not for them! A youth group would have been a better setting for that illustration.

I travel a great deal in my ministry. Over the next few months I will preach in every corner of the UK as well as in Hungary, Australia and Italy. While I love preaching in my own church most of all, I have found that preaching in different places has been a great help to me precisely because it forces me to ask questions about the people to whom am preaching. Often preachers do a great deal of thinking about the passage they are preaching on but not so much thinking about who they are preaching to. When I am in Hungary in a couple of months I will be preaching to a group of students. They are young, bright, ambitious and very well read. When I go to Australia I will be at a conference preaching to church leaders, many of whom are in very difficult situations trying to encourage growth in struggling churches. When I get to Italy it will be young people again, many from very working class families where unemployment and poverty are commonplace. In each of these situations my audience will be quite different and there will be the need to tailor my message, including my illustrations, to the particular needs of each group of people.

Illustrations that embarrass

Another mistake is to use illustrations that could potentially embarrass members of your audience. It seems almost inconceivable that this would ever be the case but I have seen it happen. I remember on one occasion a preacher using a humorous illustration which involved a fat person who was struggling to climb the stairs. Had he used this illustration subtly it might have been alright but instead he thought it would be funny to generally make fun of people who were overweight. Unfortunately several people in the audience were overweight and some were depressed about being so and consequently they were profoundly embarrassed.

It can also be embarrassing to use illustrations about people that the audience know personally, especially if it involves a negative comment associated with that person. I have even witnessed a preacher talking about a person in the audience and divulging things that person said to the preacher which the person would not have wanted anyone else to know about. This too can be very embarrassing. Of course it is not always inappropriate to use illustrations that involve people in the audience. I have often done this in my own church but my illustration will always show the person in a positive or sympathetic light and I will have either talked to the person beforehand to get their permission or will know them well enough to know that they will not be embarrassed.

Illustrations that are clumsy

Finally we need to be careful not to use illustrations that are simply clumsy because they can cause more harm than good. A clumsy illustration is one that is self-defeating because it just doesn't help the sermon. For example. I have heard illustrations being used that are so complicated that the preacher has to explain what the illustration actually means. Likewise I have seen preachers using very long illustrations that end up boring the audience. It is much more effective to use illustrations that are short and punchy. When Jesus told the Parable of the Lost Coin he did so in just 73 words. This is a brilliant example of a brief but powerful illustration used by a master communicator!

Also when you use quotations as illustrations make sure you know whose quotation is it and tell the audience who first said it. If the person being quoted is not known to the audience state briefly who they are as that also adds weight to the illustration. If you don't do this the audience will be thinking about who the mystery person might be rather than concentrating on what you want to say.

Above all, if you quote facts in an illustration make sure to get them right; it is very clumsy not to. I once made this mistake at church in my own town. I was preaching on the power of the Holy Spirit from 2 Timothy 1:6—8 and wanted to make the point that we as Christians have this great power available to us yet we often do not use it. To illustrate my point I talked about walking along the sea front in Marseilles, France on a stormy day and being impressed by the sheer power of the sea. I then said that I was surprised that some of this great energy was not captured as a power source using technology such as tidal power generation. Someone pointed out afterwards that the Mediterranean does not have tides. Actually he was not entirely correct as the Mediterranean does have tides but they are very small due to the narrow connection with the Atlantic Ocean. Nevertheless I should have known better than to use an illustration on subject I knew so little about. Always make sure when using factual illustrations that you really do know what you are talking about

And finally...

Illustrations are such an important component in preaching that it is a good habit to continually think of what would make a good illustration. I have a friend who is a very experienced preacher and he deliberately takes note of good illustrations. If he has read an interesting story in a newspaper or magazine he will cut it about and keep it. If he sees an advertisement on a billboard or on TV that would make a good illustration he makes a note of it. Whenever he comes across a poem, a proverb or even an event in his own life that would be a good illustration, it too would be noted. He may not use it in his next sermon but sooner or later a use will be found for virtually every illustration that he has collected.

It is important to remember the value of creativity. Never be afraid to use any illustration provided you don't fall into any of the traps listed above. Use your imagination and vary the kind of illustrations that you use. You might even want to use a physical action for an illustration. I once spoke on the final few verses of Isaiah 40 and wanted to make the point that we need to 'wait on God' but in our busy lives, although many of us do not find this an easy thing to do. To emphasize the point I suddenly stopped speaking and simply looked out at my audience, smiling occasionally. I did this for no longer than sixty seconds but I could see that people were already nervous and not sure where to look. Finally I said, 'It's uncomfortable isn't it, just sitting in silence and just waiting'. That illustration hammered home the point and was effective even though I didn't say a word.

Learn to be creative. Pepper your sermons with good illustrations and they will develop life, vitality and clarity that will help your audience to really appreciate what you are trying to communicate.

CHAPTER 10

Seeking Assistance:
The use of media in communication

Stephen McQuoid

When I first became a Christin one of the things I had to get used to, was being part of a church family. In time I came to love being part of church and it certainly has been a major part of my life. At the beginning, however, church was a strange world that was confusing and surprising in equal measure.

Of all the things that took time to acclimatise to, preaching was at the very top of the list. The thought of sitting quietly for thirty minutes and listening to a monologue was not my idea of fun. In fairness some of the preachers I listened to were very good. As a young Christian I didn't understand everything they were saying but they were enthusiastic — sometimes charming and often with finely-honed communications skills. Others were just dull. I remember one preacher in particular who was probably a very nice man but when he got into the pulpit his monotone voice, lifeless posture, miserable face and general lack of imagination made listening to his sermons an act of grim endurance.

At the same time that I was getting used to going to church, I was also reading my Bible and I discovered an incredible truth — many of the preachers in the Bible were highly creative communicators and they would often use the most unconventional and dramatic methods to get their message across. Ezekiel was a good example of this. He verbally communicated God's message but also did drama, used props and even used bizarre actions such a shaving himself with a sword. The lesson from this is obvious: we should feel free as preachers to use any method that will help us communicate our message effectively.

Before we think of the different methods we can utilise there should be some words of warning. Firstly be careful not use gimmicks. Creativity is good but only when it genuinely assists the job of communication. No method should ever take over from the primary aim of communicating God's word to people. I have known preachers who have fallen so much in love with power point, drama and video clips that they have forgotten their job is to be a mouthpiece for God and to explain what the text means. Use every effective method but remember your ultimate goal is not to be experimental; it is to make the word of God known.

Secondly it is important to ask the fundamental and personal question, do any of these methods work for me? This is a genuine question because we each approach the job of preaching with our own personalities and that will mean that whatever works for one person will not necessarily work for another. The key thing is to do what we are comfortable with and not feel pressurised into using some method that we are not comfortable with.

I have a friend who is a very effective pastor and an excellent preacher. He doesn't use power point or any other 'preaching aid'. He is much more comfortable just preaching and his preaching is excellent. He is confident enough in his ministry not to feel pressurised into using different media though he realises that less experienced preachers do feel the pressure and give into it in some cases to the detriment of their preaching. He sometimes he jokes with me about the situation saying that his preaching couldn't possibly be blessed by the Holy Spirit as he doesn't use power point. Behind the humour is a serious point: we should do what we do well and not use media we are not comfortable with just because others think we should. Just remember that God can use your personality so that your preaching will be unique because it is an expression of who you are. Some of the greatest preachers in history relied only on God and their own God-given ability to preach and that was enough (see p.34).

Thirdly, it is important to remember that whatever technology is out there, there is still something very powerful about one impassioned human being communicating on a personal level to another. Different preachers may have different styles but our voices, our facial expressions and our body language communicate volumes and those assets must be used in preaching. I frequently use teaching aids like power point and YouTube clips in communication but sometimes I just put away my computer and preach my heart out to people and that in itself can be deeply refreshing and powerful in our technological age.

Power point

Having sounded those words of warning we now need to ask what different methods are useful in our communication? Perhaps we should start by mentioning some of the electronic media that we have at our disposal, the most common of which is power point. This is an excellent medium for communication but one that needs to be used wisely. Sometimes when preachers use power point they have far too many slides and therefore the audience are looking more at the screen than they are at the preacher which can actually be counterproductive. The emotional connection between the preacher and his audience is important and this can only be made when they engage with him as a person. Just staring at a screen will not allow for this.

Some preachers also fall into the trap of having too many words on each slide. If people in the audience are too busy reading, they will not be able to fully concentrate on what the preacher is actually saying. As a general rule there should be no more than 25 words on each slide. After all, the job of a preacher is to preach, not to get people to read.

When using power point I tend to apply a few simple guidelines. Firstly make the power point presentation visually attractive. This can be done by use of colour, good designs, animation and good images. Secondly, when it comes to the use of images, whether photographs, drawings or symbols, choose them very carefully. The images you paste on your power point slides are not there just to fill up space, they should communicate something in themselves. There is a saying that states 'a good picture is worth a thousand words'. This is certainly true when you use pictures that help to communicate a message. Thirdly, don't have too many slides. For an average half hour sermon I would have a maximum of 5 or 6 slides as too much activity on the screen can be a distraction. Finally be careful about the kind of font you use. If the font is not easy to read it will distract the audience from listening to you as the preacher. Do not allow power point to become your master. Use it as a tool and it will greatly help in the job of preaching.

Video clips

Another form of electronic media that is very useful is video clips which these days are easy to get hold of and often are free. They don't need to be produced by some Christian media company in order to be useful— a wide range of different kinds of video clip can be used and can greatly assist your sermon if carefully used. Again a word of warning needs to be mentioned and this is a very practical one. If you choose to use a video clip, just make sure you can use this medium in a smooth and seamless way and that means checking your equipment. There is nothing worse than things going wrong and having to issue an apology when you should be preaching.

One friend of mine was preaching in a church he had never been to before and decided to make use of a video clip. It was a good one that would have been an effective tool for communication but unfortunately he had not set up all the equipment properly. He got to the point in his sermon where he was going to use the clip and introduced it to the audience by saying, 'just watch this short clip'. Unfortunately nothing happened. He stood there for a few seconds, no doubt feeling embarrassed and pressing buttons on the remote control in his hand which was supposed to control the equipment— still nothing. He then walked to the back of the church where the technical team operated the audio visual equipment and tried to find out what the problem was. After a few more seconds they managed to get everything going and the clip was shown but any momentum in his preaching was lost and the audience were too embarrassed to concentrate properly. The lesson is obvious. If you are going to complicate things by adding video material just make sure it is done properly.

As you think about how to use video clips there are a number of things you should have in the back of your mind. Firstly chose carefully. A good video clip is powerful if it adds to what you are doing but it really does need to add something. There is no point using a clip that just reproduces what you can already do. I saw this recently when a preacher introduced a video clip which was nothing more than a Bible college lecturer doing an exposition of a verse.

This was a needless interruption of the person's sermon. However if the preacher had shown an appropriate video clip from a movie or a TV documentary it would have been a genuine addition to what he was doing in his sermon.

The length of the clip is also important. Too short and it is probably not worth using, too long and it can be a distraction. This is where some editing has to come in so that you use the clip well. Often the clip will be an extract from a longer programme, for example a movie. It is important to start it at the right place and ensure that you have timed things properly so as to finish at the correct place also. One preacher was using a clip from a movie because a line that one of the actors spoke was very telling and fitted well into the point he was making in his sermon. However he had not timed things properly and he showed more than just the clip he wanted to use so his audience were 'treated' to a murder scene in the movie which he never intended to show. On another occasion a preacher wanted to show a TV advert which illustrated his point and again he let the whole thing run on too long so his audience saw the advert as well as the beginning of the next programme on the TV which was a football match. No harm was done but the audience found this funny and it proved a little distracting.

It is also important to ask when a clip should be shown. It might be used at the beginning, during, or at the end of the sermon. Whenever it is shown the audience should easily be able to see why the preacher is using it. The message of the clip must be appropriate to the point being made. There may also be the need to explain why the clip is being used and introduce it to the audience. If all this is done carefully and well it can greatly enhance the sermon.

Drama

An alternative to using video clips is to use drama as part of the sermon. The preacher himself might do the drama or he could use others to do it. If there is an element of surprise it can add to the power of the illustration. I once heard a powerful sermon during a wedding ceremony. The preacher was talking about the need for married couples to love each other and commit to the marriage vows they have made before God. He stated that in any relationship there can be interruptions that can be damaging and need to be dealt with. Suddenly a mobile phone could be heard ringing and a member of the audience answered their phone and began a loud phone conversation during the sermon. This was all pre-arranged and visually demonstrated the point being made.

Role Play

Yet another thing that you can utilise is role play, though this is risky and you need to be sure of your audience. Essentially role play involves using members of the audience in a simulated situation so that they can both see and even experience what is being taught. A friend of mine uses this method very effectively, though interestingly, he does not use it very often just in case of overkill. On one occasion while teaching through the gospel of Luke he came to chapter 15 which tells of the story of the prodigal son. He decided to tell the story but also use it as a role play. He asked an elderly man in the congregation to stand up and imagine he was the father in the story. Then he chose a couple of young men to be the brothers, one of whom ran away to squander the father's wealth. Other members of the audience were called upon to play other minor roles. Once the role play finished the preacher asked the three main characters to describe how they felt about what had happened in the story. Their description enabled him to convey the emotion of the text as he preached.

First person narrative preaching

Finally there is what could be described as First Person Narrative Preaching. This is when the preacher becomes one of the characters in the story. I have only ever done this once, though it worked well and would try again if the situation was appropriate. It is not an easy method because it is a bit like doing a one-man drama. The time I did it I was preaching from 1 Samuel 17 which is the story of David's battle with Goliath. I wanted to emphasize both the great challenge that Goliath posed for the Israelites and also the courage and faith in God that David had as he confronted the frightening giant. I knew that the congregation would know the story of David and Goliath well so I used this method to add a different and surprising twist. I took the place of King Saul who was too afraid to fight Goliath and, pretending to be him, I told the audience how ashamed I felt that I didn't have the confidence in God to do what should be done and expressed my shock that David, the young boy, did have that confidence. This is not an easy method of preaching but if used sparingly can be very effective and absorbing.

Each of these methods, and others, have their place in preaching. However it is important always to remind yourself that while creativity is good, any method that we utilise should assist the sermon and not distract attention from it. We should use things that bring clarity, precision, explanation or a sense of the emotion of the Bible passage. If these methods do this they are worth using. However, we need to be discerning and not just utilise these things for the sake of it.

CHAPTER 11

Feeding the flock:
Establishing a healthy teaching programme

Jeremy McQuoid

School dinners in the UK have changed a lot since I was a boy. Thirty years ago when I went to the school canteen, we were served with almost the same dishes every day: chicken and chips, beef casserole and chips, something resembling mincemeat with chips. It is a wonder that I haven't died of a heart attack yet!

However a few years ago, Jamie Oliver, a celebrity chef who appears regularly on British television, went on a tour of British schools and was shocked to find UK children being exposed to such unhealthy food and bad diets. He was so incensed that he put together a television series that has revolutionised the kind of food our children eat today.

Now my children bring me home a full menu for a month of school dinners. This menu contains about ten different dishes a week, plenty of fruit and vegetables, and the menu even tells you the calorie content of each meal so that you can give your children a healthy, balanced diet. How times have changed!

A balanced biblical diet

If it is important to have a balanced diet in the physical world, how much more so in the spiritual world. In this chapter we want to lay out the importance of a carefully-planned, systematic teaching programme that will feed, nourish and mature the church for generations to come.

The word 'diet' is very biblical. The Scriptures present Bible teaching quite often through the imagery of eating and food. We need to 'feed' our people on 'green pasture'. A young Christian needs 'milk' to begin with, but after a while needs to progress to more solid, meaty teaching. Our whole spiritual health and vitality as individuals and as churches depends so much on what kind of diet we are being given from the pulpit.

So how do we feed and nourish our people towards Christian maturity?

A Programme?

Some preachers are sceptical about any thought of a preaching plan. Charles Spurgeon, for example, the greatest preacher of his age, strongly disagreed with the notion of preaching through a Bible book. He wanted to be open to the Spirit's leading to such an extent that he never knew what he was going to speak on from one Sunday to the next!

There seems to be an understanding in some Christian circles that being led by the Spirit, and having a preaching plan are mutually exclusive. But I cannot agree. The Holy Spirit, the ultimate author of Scripture, has put together such a coherent storyline in the Bible that part of a week-by-week preacher's duty must surely be to show that coherence by preaching systematically through books of the Bible.

I am currently preaching through a series on the book of Hebrews. The book has a clear structure. It is an exposition of the supremacy of Christ - how he is superior to angels; superior to Moses; to Joshua; to the Aaronic priesthood. There is a strong flow of logic throughout the book.

And when that coherent argument has reached a powerful conclusion at the end of chapter 10, the writer applies that teaching by telling his readers to live by faith (ch. 11) and to 'run with perseverance the race marked out for us' (Heb.12: 1). The power of the book builds with every passage and reaches a crescendo in chapters 11 and 12. That is how the Holy Spirit has inspired the writer to set out his book.

The same is true of most other books of the Bible. They do not simply tell stories of Jesus or display wise sayings thrown together at random. Biblical criticism during the last century has shown more than ever that each book has its own logical flow and development. The power of each book can only be felt when a preacher unpacks that book systematically.

If you read Ephesians, even in one sitting, you will see that in the first 3 chapters, Paul is setting out the doctrine of the church — God's plan to set apart a people from himself who will display God's glory to the cosmic powers. Then after you have preached that powerful, inspiring doctrine, the practical teaching of the second half of the book, beginning in chapter 4 with Paul urging us to 'live a life worthy of the calling you have received', is all the more impactful (Eph. 4: 1).

The practical commands Paul gives —for husbands to love their wives, and slaves to obey their masters, for example — enable us to fulfil God's glorious vision for his church. Chapters 4 to 6 are not commands placed in a vacuum, but deliberately set against the backdrop of God's cosmic plan to build a church for his glory from chapters 1 to 3.

But if you don't preach through Ephesians, and simply pick out the passage about wives and husbands, it can come across as pure legalism, passing on a series of individual commands ripped from their original context, as if all God wants us to do is to obey moral instructions. With that kind of constant 'diet' of passages ripped from their context, Christians can easily slide into 'works righteousness' — the idea that all we need to do is keep obeying God's rules to be good Christians and the doctrine of grace is removed.

Spirit-driven preaching programmes

The clearest way you can truly preach the Word, as the Spirit intended, is to work your way systematically, passage by passage and book by book, seeing every verse and paragraph and chapter in its wider context. That does not diminish the work of the Spirit but allows us to hear the words of God as the Spirit intended them to be heard.

Even though I know what passage in Hebrews I will be preaching next week, I pray no less urgently for the Spirit to inspire my preaching than someone who is waiting for the Spirit to reveal the right text to them. I ask the Spirit:

Lord, show me the meaning of this text, its hidden depths.

Show me how this passage follows on from the previous passage.

Show me how to apply this passage in a relevant, personal and gripping way

to my hearers who need me to bring the word of God to impact their lives today.

Grant me clear illustrations to shed light on the truths of the passage and prepare the hearts of those who will listen to not only be hearers of the Word but doers also.

Create within them a growing hunger for your truth.

May the full impact of this Scripture passage achieve what you desire it to achieve in our hearts just as you led the original author to pen these words.

And when I get up to speak, anoint my lips to speak with power beyond human words.

Systematic preaching through a book does not remove the Spirit from the preaching. It actually increases my excitement that the Spirit who inspired the writer to write wants to take those words and thoughts and coherent arguments to inspire people in the same way today.

Preaching what people need, not what they want

Working your way through Bible books, passage by passage, also protects you from telling people what they want to hear. A large number of preaching programmes today are based on 'felt needs.' We put topical series together about 'how to be a better parent' or 'dealing with money.'

They are, of course, helpful topics that are immediately relevant. But preachers often end up looking for 'proof texts' to help them say what they want to say about these subjects and what they think people want to hear. It is one step removed from declaring what the Holy Spirit has placed in Scripture because you inevitably do not deal with verses in their context. You end up with a preacher preaching worldly wisdom and attaching some Bible verses to his sermon to make the message sound biblical.

What constantly amazes me about Bible exposition, on the other hand, is that God rarely wants to talk about what we want to talk about. I come to church wanting to know how to be a better parent or how to deal with bereavement but God wants to tell me about Christ and sin and salvation. About getting ready for judgement and living a holy life today. The whole prophetic purpose of the Bible is to take us away from human thinking in order to expose us to divine priorities.

We always want to pray 'give us today our daily bread', when God actually wants our primary passion to be 'hallowed be YOUR NAME. YOUR KINGDOM come. Your will be done. (Mt.6:9—13)'. The Lord's Prayer does, on a small scale, what the Bible does on a large scale. It takes us away from an obsession with our felt needs and gives us a God-centred worldview.

A preaching programme that displays God's priorities

So if we are convinced that the best way to mature God's people is to preach passage by passage and book by book, how exactly should we go about that? After all, there are 66 books in the Bible — a lot of material.

One important principle to remember is that while all scripture is God's truth, it is not all equally important. Scripture itself teaches us this. When Paul is telling the Corinthians the facts behind the Gospel, he says to them:

> Now, brothers and sisters, I want to remind you of the gospel
> I preached to you, which you received and on which you
> have taken your stand…For what I received I passed on
> to you AS OF FIRST IMPORTANCE [author's capitals]:
> that Christ died for our sins according to the Scriptures' (1
> Cor 15:1—3NIV).

If you read through the first letter to the Corinthians, Paul has to deal with a lot of minor issues. In an immature church where there was leadership rivalry, believers were taking each other to court and the abuse of charismatic gifts was leading to chaos in the church.

But in chapter 15 Paul gets to what he really wants to talk about —the Gospel, centred on the death, burial and resurrection of Christ. This is more important than leadership in the church, or moral failings in the community, or the use of spiritual gifts.

So a wise preaching programme will emphasize those books in Scripture that most clearly define the Gospel of Jesus Christ. Ecclesiastes and Romans are two books from Scripture of similar length but a wise preaching programme will place more emphasis on Romans than on Ecclesiastes, because Romans is the clearest explanation of the Gospel in the whole of Scripture. That is the purpose of the book.

The magisterial books

With this principle in mind, it is difficult to imagine putting a preaching programme together for the health and vitality of the church without emphasizing what we might call the 'magisterial books': the books of Old and New Testament that most clearly emphasize the Gospel. These could be listed as follows

- **Genesis** tells us about the creation of the Universe, the loving relationship God originally intended between himself and man, the fall into sin, and the beginning of God's plan of salvation. It would be difficult to imagine a preaching plan over 10 years in a church that did not spend good time in Genesis.
- **Exodus** contains the story of the Passover and is the 'salvation story' of the Old Testament which points so clearly to the cross and redemption 'through the blood of the lamb' (Ex.12:7 cf 1Pet.1:19). Meanwhile the 10 commandments are so pivotal in understanding both God's holy character and how far we fall short of God's standards. Paul said in Galatians 'the law was our guardian until Christ came' (Ex. 20: 1—17 cf. Gal.3: 24).
- **Numbers** continues the story of Israel, moving through the wilderness to the Promised Land. There are so many 'core' Gospel themes in this book. The holiness of God, his judgement on sin, his grace to rebels. Israel's journey through the wilderness mirrors a Christian's journey from salvation to glory.
- **1 and 2 Samuel** plot the rise of kingship in Israel. Who can be the ideal king who will lead God's people to victory? David is Israel's best king, yet

his sinful act with Bathsheba shows that God's people still need to await the ultimate king who can free them from sin and lead them to glory.

- **Psalms** – carefully selected Psalms point to a coming Messiah and teach us how to worship God as believers in the midst of the trials and temptations of life.
- **Isaiah** – the prophetic books are hard to preach but Isaiah is such a rich book. It highlights Israel's sin and need of a Saviour, points to a coming Messiah who would be both King and Suffering Servant, and highlights the ultimate destiny of peace and glory for those who submit to God's Messiah. Isaiah is Gospel from start to finish.
- **The Gospels** – Clearly any gospel-driven preaching plan must spend significant time in the Gospels. I have found Mark an excellent gospel to work your way through, as it presents the basic thrust of Jesus' life and ministry, the meaning of the cross, and the call to his hearers to 'take up their cross and follow me' (Mk. 8.34). The Gospel is more than just believing — it is living a cross-centred life.
- **Acts** – a unique book showing the kind of preaching and divine providence that moved the gospel from Jerusalem to Rome in 30 years. We are living in Acts chapter 29 today, with an ongoing call to take this Gospel across the globe.
- **Romans** – the book which sets out the message of the Gospel in the most systematic way. You cannot have a 10-year preaching programme that avoids this pivotal book – especially chapters 1 to 8 where Paul uncovers humanity's need of a Saviour; the cross as God's response, justification by faith, sanctification, life in the Spirit, and the hope of glory. Romans is a mini systematic theology and it is worth all the effort it takes to unpack. Romans 8 especially sets out the Gospel from start to finish. A 3 or 4 part series in Romans 8 would be extremely beneficial.
- **Ephesians** – a book which unveils God's plans for his church from eternity to eternity and discusses the vital issue of spiritual warfare.
- **Hebrews** – Hebrews and Romans are the two great 'Bible overview' books. To study Hebrews is to see how Old and New Testaments come together in the person of Jesus Christ. It hones in on the new covenant

in Christ's blood (Heb. 12:24) and Jesus' priestly ministry for us in heaven while calling us practically to live by faith.
- **Revelation** – be careful with Revelation, but don't ignore it as it is surprisingly practical. It focuses on the ultimate victory of Christ and the call to persevere until he returns in glory.

A balanced diet

If the magisterial books form a solid 'core' to your teaching programme, it is also important to give a balance of 'genres.' We need to expose God's people to the various ways he speaks. Genesis is mostly narrative storytelling. The Psalms are poetry. Exodus contains legal documents alongside narrative. Isaiah is a mixture of prophecy and poetry. The Gospels are biography and contain the fascinating genre of 'parable'. Acts is history and then we have the New Testament letters.

I find it helpful to move from one genre to another and from one Testament to another. If I've been in Genesis for a while, I might move to Romans or Ephesians to provide some freshness to the preaching programme. Then to parables of Jesus or some carefully chosen Psalms. It is important not to get stuck in a rut.

A friend of mine told me that when he went to study at University, the church he attended was beginning a series on the book of Acts. My friend spent 4 years at university and when he finished the church was still on Acts! While that preacher was no doubt committed to expository preaching, he was failing to give his people a balanced diet.

God did not make his word monotonal, still less monotonous. We need to feel the emotion of biblical poetry, the ambiguity of biblical history, the 'sting in the tale' of parables, the exactitude of legal requirements, the directness of prophecy, and the bizarre pictures of apocalyptic literature so that we preach the Word in its fullness and variety.

Don't prolong preaching series

It is helpful, as a general rule, not to spend too long on one series. Your people need to hear what Paul called 'the whole counsel of God', (Acts 20: 27) and if you spend half your life on Romans or Hebrews or Luke's Gospel, wonderful texts though they are, your church will get bored, or they will feel the Bible is all about justification by faith, or the life of Jesus when there is so much more to discover.

A wise preacher will come out of his longer series on Genesis or Matthew to preach a brief series on suffering from Job; or the meaning of life from Ecclesiastes. I often find holiday periods are a good time to look at these more philosophical books that show the full spectrum of life experience.

Michael Eton, a pastor from Nairobi, who also has experience of preaching in numerous countries says that a good series lasts for about thirteen Sundays. It is not too short to be superficial or easily forgotten and not too long to get bogged down. Personally, I don't stick to that idea rigidly. I have done twenty sessions in a series but I don't want to do much more than twenty before looking for a new genre and fresh material to bring to my people.

It's also important to test yourself as a preacher. I feel most comfortable preaching through logical letters like Romans but it does my own soul good to stretch myself with some poetry and prophecy. If you are preaching for a long time, it is possible to get bored with your own preaching so moving out of your 'comfort zone' can freshen your ministry. If you are bored, chances are your listeners will be as well.

Let the passage dictate

You may feel that I have not given topical preaching a fair hearing. I am not against topical preaching but often I find when I am given a topic, I want to find a text that matches the topic. I find myself wanting to make the passage say what it does not really say so that I can preach the topic rather than the text!

Don't ever bend a passage to make it fit a topic! The safest approach and closest to how the Spirit has put together Scripture is to move passage by passage and book by book, mixing up genres, spending fifteen or so sessions on any one series and never straying far from the gospel and the cross.

If you keep these principles in mind, you will provide a balanced biblical diet to feed your people. You will be training them how to read the Bible for themselves. You will not be faddish in your preaching but constantly drawing people back to God's eternal Word and you will be communicating to people what God has eternally spoken in the precise way he has spoken it. That is the pathway to spiritual maturity in your flock and, as a by-product, you will immerse yourself in Scripture and get to know God better.

CHAPTER 12

The power of integrity:
What turns an orator into a mouthpiece for God

Stephen McQuoid

It was a scandal that shocked a nation. Conrad De Suza, a 53-year-old Tanzanian-born man, was jailed after standing trial for pretending to be a doctor. De Suza had attended medical school in the early 1980s but dropped out without qualifying. However, he lied about his lack of qualifications and was employed by Lewisham Council in London as a medical advisor for more than 10 years. To the outside world he appeared to be a doctor but when the truth finally caught up with him he lost all credibility and the respect of anyone who knew him.

The great fourth century preacher, John Chrysostom, once compared preaching to medical intervention. He said it had the effect of dealing with spiritual sickness and providing a cure. This is true, but in much the same way that Conrad De Suza turned out to be a fraud, any preacher who lacks integrity will find that his ministry is greatly affected and his spiritual medicine less potent. Merely speaking words is not enough if they are not backed up by a life that says, 'I am qualified to say these things'. Not that we expect preachers to be perfect! No preacher will be. But every preacher should believe in what he preaches and be determined to live out in his own life what he asks of others. After all, why would anyone listen to a preacher who says one thing and does another, or who preaches about God's transforming power and yet lives a life that is clearly not transformed? Such a preacher is a fraud and a hypocrite. So what is it that gives a preacher real integrity? What makes the difference between his merely being an orator and his being a mouthpiece for God? What pitfalls should he avoid as he endeavours to proclaim the word of God?

The first thing that gives a preacher integrity is having pure motives in all that he does. The issue of motives is a big one because as fallen human beings we are all capable of doing the right thing for entirely the wrong reason. The purity of our hearts may not easily be seen by our congregation, but God sees and his approval of our ministry is the most important thing. It is a healthy thing to keep questioning our motives so that we are clear about why we preach.

The real danger here is that preachers preach simply to be heard. Preachers are the centre of attention when they preach. All eyes are on them and people listen to their every word. If they are not careful this can inflate their egos and they can preach, not to glorify God, but rather to be heard and admired. A friend of mine made a comment about his pastor saying that his pastor's best friend was the pulpit. By that he meant that the thing his pastor most valued was to be up front, in the public eye, and to be listened to. I knew the pastor he was talking about and was saddened to discover that when the pastor retired from his job, he became a very unhappy man. He was unhappy because he no longer had that profile, that status, and he was no longer in a position to have an audience to speak to and be heard by. The adulation he enjoyed as a pastor was like a drug. It motivated him and gave him a craving for more. The attention he received from his audience was what he preached for rather than the glory of God.

Pride is such a danger for preachers. If preachers are not careful they can allow themselves to become minor celebrities rather that humble servants of God. I am always interested to observe preachers as they mingle socially with members of their congregation. It is revealing to see what they talk about. Do they talk about themselves and their ministries, or do they show an interest in the lives of those they are ministering to? Are they enjoying the praise of their audience, or do they show real pastoral care? Are they people who want to receive, or are they people who want to give? I am always very suspicious when a preacher asks a member of the congregation whether they enjoyed the sermon. Is it because they want to know if God was speaking to the person or is it simply because they are looking for approval or affirmation?

For me this is not just an academic issue for I have to question my own motives. I preach every week, not just in my own church but in many other churches. In some churches it is the norm for the preacher to stand at the door of the church at the end of the service and shake everyone's hand as they leave. Often when this happens people give compliments about the sermon and thank the preacher for what he has said. When I am in this situation I have to remind myself, as well as the person I am speaking to, that if there has been blessing and encouragement as a result of the sermon then it is to the glory of God alone. After all, I can only speak because God gave me a tongue. I can only think through the content of my sermon because God gave me a brain and I can only challenge people because God has given his Holy Spirit in power to transform their hearts. Any positive effect has little to do with me and everything to do with God. I dare not accept any praise or be deluded into thinking that I am anything more than a mouthpiece for God to speak through.

Pride in the pulpit can have several very ugly manifestations. One is that the preacher can begin to feel that he is an entertainer. Of course, there is nothing wrong with a preacher being easy to listen to, humorous, absorbing and even fun. Good communicators will use all sorts of methods to hold the attention of their audience and God has gifted many of the preachers that I know with the ability to make their audience smile, laugh, cry and remember all that has been said. However, the primary goal of the preacher should not be to entertain, to be funny or even to be interesting. His primary goal should be to declare God's Word to those who listen. If this is done in an entertaining way it is valid, but danger lurks! Preachers with a pride problem want to be popular. They want people to love them and to what to hear what they have to say. There is a huge temptation to avoid challenging their audience and instead just present them with an enjoyable sermon. This is dangerous not least because it is a misuse of the gift God has given us.

Another ugly manifestation of pride is when a preacher just tells his audience what they want to hear. Paul warned Timothy about this (2 Tim. 4: 3) saying that preachers can preach in such a way that they allow their audiences to live any way they like. Of course, it may well be that when we preach we often say things that are encouraging, but sermons are not primarily about the 'feel good' factor. It would be tempting to tell our congregations that the sins they commit are not too bad, or that God doesn't judge people or send them to hell. It would make life easier for the preacher if he did not need to declare God's ethical standards or challenge people about holiness, commitment and servanthood. It would be nice to be able to tell church members that they can keep all their money to themselves without feeling guilty; they don't need to give anything to the poor; they can avoid all hardship and never have to surrender to the will of God. However, such preaching would not be faithful. It would not be consistent with Scripture and it would not honour God.

As well as having pure motives, preachers also need to have a strong sense of personal responsibility if they are to have integrity in their ministry. The job of preaching is an important one and it needs to be taken seriously. No preacher who values the Bible and desires transformation in the lives of those he speaks to will do anything less than his very best as he fulfils his ministry. If our congregation does not believe we are deeply committed to the task of preaching they will not really listen to what we have to say. After all, why should they take our ministry seriously if we don't? It is important therefore that we work hard at our preparation. Many years ago, I attended a church where the pastor was a highly able and articulate man. However, he could often be seen scribbling notes on some scraps of paper as he sat through the worship section of the service before getting up to deliver his message. Often it was apparent that he had not done much preparation other than those hurriedly scribbled notes and the impact on the congregation was equally evident. Most felt that what he said could not be particularly important as clearly he had not spent time immersed in God's Word so that he would have something to offer. Evidently he had ability but did not gain the respect of those who listened.

Preachers who have a strong sense of responsibility will not only prepare themselves by studying, but also by praying and calling upon God to speak powerfully through them. That commitment to prayer will add real weight to what they say. It will be evident that they are not just saying words and making statements, rather they are preaching about things they passionately believe in and with the deeply felt desire that God would take their words and change hearts.

If a preacher has a strong sense of personal responsibility in his ministry, he will be both honest and courageous. He will be willing to say things that are hard and things that are unpopular. He will value truth and its declaration more that he values the comfort of his audience. Recently I was preaching on a passage in the New Testament that talks about adultery and I was very conscious that there were two people in the congregation who were committing adultery. It was not an easy passage to preach from and there was an almost overwhelming temptation skip over the most difficult verses so as to avoid the embarrassment of the two people concerned who were, incidentally, friends of mine. However it would have been cowardly and dishonest to do so. Certainly I could not have claimed to be honouring God or valuing the privilege of preaching if I had taken the easy way out. The congregation, including the two people whose lifestyle the passage was examining, would not have respected my ministry had I done so. I hope I spoke with gentleness and compassion, but I know that I also had to bring the truth of God's Word to that situation.

Recently I had the privilege of visiting a church whose pastor had just retired after many years of ministry. He was not the most dynamic of men and in all honesty his style of preaching was fairly old-fashioned and often dull. However, it was obvious that his congregation had the highest regard for him as a preacher as well as a Christian leader and that they had been blessed by his ministry over the years. One member of the congregation told me that the reason she felt this way about him was because everything he did demonstrated a deep commitment to the Bible, his congregation, prayer and his preaching ministry. His great sense of personal responsibility had compelled him to give his all and his congregation listened to him and responded because of it.

It goes without saying that preachers need to live out their faith and that this is a key to their integrity. There is an old adage that says, 'You should practise what you preach'. This is true for all kinds of reasons. James tells us that those who put themselves in the position of being teachers will be judged more harshly (Jas 3: 1). The reason for this is that God holds us accountable for our actions and sinning is bad, but to sin in the context of an issue you have preached about, and in which you have demanded of others a high standard, is doubly wrong. God scrutinises the lives of those who have the awesome responsibility of handling and declaring his Word. If what we say is nothing more than just words that are not backed up by action, then God will deal with us.

One of the ways God deals with us is by withdrawing his blessing from what we do so that our preaching ceases to be impacting and life-changing. We need to remember that if we don't practice what we preach those who listen will understandably have a negative view of what we say. After all, if I preach about holiness and yet do not live a holy life, or if I preach about being surrendered to the will of God and yet my own life rebels against it, those who hear me preaching will be utterly unimpressed with what I say. It is repulsive to hear someone demanding standards of others that the person who is making the demands, is not willing to live up to. It is hypocritical and shallow and will not lead to vibrant growth in the church.

Of course, no church will expect its preachers to be perfect and no preacher ever will be. We are at best failing human beings who struggle to please God. However, there is a big difference between someone who preaches about God's standards and works hard to live up to them and someone who preaches those same messages and shows little interest in being the person God wants him to be. As we preach we need to remember that we too are under the authority of God's Word and that it applies to us. Our first priority is to ensure that we are being changed and only then can we look for transformation in the lives of those we preach to. I have always made it my habit to ask God to speak to me first through the passage I am studying before I preach it to my congregation. This habit has been a blessing because in nearly thirty years of preaching, I have never once preached a passage of Scripture that did not really challenge me in some way.

It should also be said that we need to be absolutely honest in our preaching and not pretend to be something we are not. This requires that we are open about our struggles and failings and do not give the impression that we have completely sorted out our lives or that we do not face temptation. Being honest and admitting to failings is not a sign of weakness, rather it is an acknowledgment that we, like everyone else, must be subject to the word of God knowing that we need the help of the Holy Spirit in order to have our lives properly shaped by it. This kind of honesty will in itself give credibility to our ministry because it will demonstrate that that we take the Bible seriously enough to want it to change our lives and not just the lives of those we preach to.

CHAPTER 13

The Anointing:
What it means to have the touch
of the Spirit in preaching

Jeremy McQuoid

In 1904, one of the most amazing revivals in church history broke out across the nation of Wales. In one year, over 100,000 men, women and children gave their lives to Christ. It is even suggested that a police station was closed so that policemen could follow new careers as there was no crime and Chapels were crowded at 3am, often with renowned town drunks crying out to God for mercy.

One of the great stories that emerged from this revival was of pit ponies who used to take the Welshmen down the mines. These ponies rebelled against their owners because they could not understand why their riders had stopped being so rough with them, but treated them with a gentleness that was a sign of the Spirit of God transforming an entire culture.

At the heart of the Welsh revival was a young preacher named Evan Roberts, who literally spent himself, body and soul, during these unusual days, travelling round Wales making passionate appeals in the power of the Spirit. Roberts was unusual because he was very young, in his mid-twenties at the time and he had no formal training. Indeed the revival had very little impact on church ministers with theology degrees!

It was not Evan Roberts' natural charisma, or accurate sermon construction, or even heart-warming illustrations that made him such a powerful preacher. It was his hunger for God.

Jonathan Edwards

Wind back another 150 years and there is the fascinating story of Jonathan Edwards, an American preacher with a brilliant mind who became President of Princeton Theological Seminary. He was a thoughtful academic with a very dull manner in the pulpit.

Edwards was so unnatural as a public speaker that his sermon notes used to include little pointers for him to use facial gestures. Yale University in the United States still has copies of some of his sermon manuscripts written in minute scribbles where he tells himself to make sure he looks up from his page to have eye contact with his congregation. By all accounts Edwards was awkward in the pulpit and very difficult to listen to.

And yet he preached a sermon that stirred one of the great revivals of Church history. His sermon was famously entitled 'Sinners in the Hands of an Angry God' — not the kind of sermon that would attract people today. But Edwards preached the truth of God's awesome final judgement with such unpolished conviction that the Spirit fell on all who attended.

Audible groans were heard as Edwards compared a sinner waiting for judgement to a spider dangling over a fire held by only the finest thread. Edwards was so full of the Holy Spirit as he preached that a spark was lit that night in Enfield, Connecticut which would become a flame of revival power across the entire eastern seaboard of the United States.

Hungry for the Spirit

The link between the young, uneducated miner's son from South Wales and the Seminary President who was too tied to his notes, was a deep walk with God and an unquenchable thirst for the power of the Spirit. Ultimately it is not our eloquence that breathes new life into peoples' souls, nor the number of hours we have spent finely crafting a sermon. It is only as the Holy Spirit takes the word of God preached from the pulpit and cuts the human heart open, with all its mixed motives and godless appetites, that anything of eternal value is achieved. If the Spirit is so central to the preaching task, we need to ask ourselves a deeply personal question that goes beyond how much we study or how well we deliver from the pulpit.

How much do we long for the Spirit's power in our own lives? How convinced are we that, without the touch of the Spirit, our words will achieve nothing however gifted we feel we are? Likewise, how deep is our expectation that our feeble words, empowered by the Spirit of God, can make the difference between heaven and hell for souls who stand on the edge of eternity? The power of the Spirit is a non-negotiable trait of effective preaching so we cannot separate the effectiveness of the preacher from his own walk with God.

The controversial Spirit

I have a bookcase full of books on biblical preaching, some of them running to 500 pages in length. These books cover every possible preaching theme. And yet it is very difficult to find a chapter or even a section of a chapter devoted to this crucial topic of Holy Spirit power in the pulpit.

I think there is a reason for that. No doubt the authors of these books all have a conviction that effective preaching demands the power of the Spirit but talk of the mysterious work of the Holy Spirit leaves many feeling uncomfortable, and unable to express in words what Spirit-filled preaching means and unwilling to enter into controversies that have brought division between so-called 'charismatic' believers and more conservative Christians.

What is 'Spirit-Filled' Preaching?

Unfortunately, many people confuse Holy Spirit power with a charismatic personality. A preacher who draws crowds with his dynamic oratory is not necessarily filled with the Spirit any more than a 'quiet' preacher who stands motionless behind a desk.

One of the most Spirit-filled preachers I have listened to is the late John Stott (1921-2011). Each time I heard him preach I sensed the deep sincerity of a man who had walked with God for many years, and there is no doubt his lips were touched by the Spirit for over 60 years of preaching ministry in all parts of the world. Many consider him the most effective biblical preacher of the twentieth century.

And yet when you watched him preach, he stood almost motionless behind the pulpit, never waving his arms about, rarely using humour, never shouting or raising his voice. He never relied on his own charisma. Stott unpacked the text like a surgeon dissecting a cadaver and then applied the text with penetrating insight and conviction to peoples' hearts. He was never a showman. The godliness of his character, allied to the depth in which he understood Scripture and believed in its power to change lives, was the secret of his Spirit-filled ministry.

Assessing a preacher's spirituality is always going to be subjective but when John Stott rose to preach, there was a stillness in the audience, almost a holy awe, because you knew you were going to hear the insights of a man who walked with God, knew God in the quiet place and was passionate about helping others know and love God as much as he did. Every time I listened to Stott preach, I left not only with a richer understanding of scripture, but asking myself, 'how can I have a walk with God as deep as this man?'

'Be Filled with the Spirit'

Robert Murray MacCheyne (1813-1843), another godly preacher famously said, 'the greatest need of my people is my own holiness'.[11] He felt he owed it to his congregation, not just to study the text in detail but to love the God of the text, to have a Christ-intoxicated heart that could not be hidden when he rose to preach 'the boundless riches of Christ' (Eph. 3: 8).

That's what we mean by 'anointing'. Some preachers talk about the anointing as if it were some special spiritual endowment God has given to chosen individuals. I have no doubt that God has set apart certain people to be unusually effective public speakers and the temptation for young preachers is often to try and copy them.

That is a dangerous thing to do. God has created you to be exactly who you are — not John Stott or John Piper or Billy Graham. Each of those men has been set aside by God to glorify him in their own ministries. Don't try to imitate them. The key to the anointing we are speaking about in this chapter

---

11 Quoted in J.I. Packer, *Rediscovering Holiness*, Ann Arbor, MI: Servant, 1992, p.32

is not to imitate a 'one-of-a-kind' preacher in your generation but to be a weak human vessel through whom God speaks powerfully.

And the key to God speaking powerfully through you is as much your own godliness, your own 'aliveness' to the Spirit, as it is any extra endowment from God or natural speaking ability. We are not responsible for gifts we don't have, but we must 'fan into flame' the gifts we do have (2 Tim. 1: 6).

The Apostle Paul realized, when speaking to the Corinthians, that he did not have the rhetorical skill of Apollos who probably had classical Greek training. I am relieved to know it was possible to fall asleep during Paul's sermons! (Acts 20:7—12). There were more gifted preachers around in Paul's day than the great apostle.

But any lack of polish or rhetorical skill in Paul was more than made up for by the zeal of a man who lived for Christ, who walked in step with the Spirit, and set Europe and Asia ablaze with his passion for God. If you read Paul's writings carefully you will find he is more passionate than polished.

In fact in 2 Corinthians he goes off on a wild tangent from chapters 2 to 7 which is what every preaching book will tell you never to do. But his Spirit-filled soul made that tangent glorious — the theme is ministry according to the Spirit not according to the law. Don't search for a more powerful technique to influence people but ensure that your preaching is the overflow of a heart that truly communes with God.

How can I be filled with the Spirit?

That very title may put you off this paragraph! I do not accept any kind of 'second blessing' scenario where a Christian needs to wait after his conversion to be baptized in the Holy Spirit. Paul is very clear that every Christian is baptized in the Spirit from the moment of conversion 'we were all baptized by one Spirit so as to form one body…and we were all given the one Spirit to drink.' (1 Cor.12: 13)

Some teachers point to the book of Acts where there was sometimes a delay between conversion and the giving of the Spirit, but many scholars have rightly pointed out that these delays were not normative but were important in allowing the Jewish church to see with their own eyes that God was pouring out his Spirit on Gentiles as well.

However, while I do not feel it is correct to speak of a post-conversion experience which we call 'baptism of the Spirit', Paul clearly commands all believers to 'be filled with the Spirit' (Eph.5: 18). The verb is in the present continuous tense – literally 'be being filled with the Spirit.' It is important for every believer, and preachers especially, to be constantly desiring and longing for a fresh filling of the Holy Spirit. And many preachers lack power in the pulpit because they do not long for the fulness of the Spirit as they preach.

We are not necessarily looking for some dramatic experience of the Spirit, though there are many examples in church history of men and women who have been overwhelmed by the power of the Spirit at pivotal times in their ministry. D. L. Moody, the great Chicago evangelist, was approached by two ladies in a Methodist Church who told him they were praying for increased power in his ministry. A short time later, while he was walking in New York, the Spirit came upon him in great power. Here is how R. A. Torrey tells the story:

> [H]e [Moody] had to hurry off to the house of a friend and ask that he might have a room by himself, and in that room he stayed alone for hours; and the Holy Ghost came upon him, filling his soul with such joy that at last he had to ask God to withhold His hand, lest he die on the spot from very joy. He went out from that place with the power of the Holy Ghost upon him, and when he got to London … the power of God wrought through him mightily in North London, and hundreds were added to the churches[12]

'Be Being Filled'

Now some may call that experience 'baptism in the Spirit'. I disagree, and we should not teach it as a normative experience that would leave millions of truly born-again Christians frustrated because that haven't 'had it'. But we are called to be filled with the Spirit, to long for that filling, to recognize that we are powerless in our preaching without our lips being touched by the Spirit. And who are we to tell the Holy Spirit of God what he can and cannot do!

---

12 R. A. Torrey, *Why God used D. L. Moody,* 1923, Section 7.
Electronic text: *https://www.wholesomewords.org/biography/biomoody6.html*

I have longed for such an experience in my ministry and never felt I was wrong to ask God for it. And there are many times in both my preaching and preparation to preach when I have felt myself 'caught up in the Spirit', when I can feel that the words have come from somewhere beyond my own intellect and abilities and where the Holy Spirit has unusually impacted a congregation.

We cannot manufacture such moments. The Spirit is sovereign in how he empowers us. But it is a fundamental part of my calling as a preacher to pray and live with such holy zeal that I become a vessel through which the Holy Spirit is pleased to move.

I am not advocating a one-off experience of the Spirit that takes away all our preaching struggle and lets us float with the angels. Such thinking is nonsense and contrary to the lives of the apostles. But I am suggesting that we can all put ourselves in a place spiritually where the Spirit is more likely to empower us.

Some practicalities

How can we do that? Murray MacCheyne said 'a holy minster is an awful weapon in the hands of God'[13] Are you holy? You will never be a weapon for God if you are not, but you can be used beyond your natural abilities if you are walking 'in step with the Spirit' (Gal.5: 25).

How disciplined is your devotional life? Many people seem to think that talk of the Spirit and daily discipline are almost contradictory. They claim that the Spirit rushes upon you and has little to do with the day-to-day grind of spiritual discipline. But it is the Spirit himself who calls us through the Word to discipline ourselves for godliness (1 Tim. 4: 8).

He is much more likely to empower our words when we have disciplined ourselves to read the Word and pray on a regular basis. But discipline does not suggest a lack of longing or passion or zeal. I find in my own heart the more disciplined I become in scripture reading and prayer, the more passionately I long for Holy Spirit power, and the more aware I am of my utter dependence on his touch from heaven.

---

13 Charles Spurgeon, *Lectures to My Students*, Carlisle: Banner of Truth, 2008, p.2.

A danger for preachers is to be always wanting to preach to others as they read a passage from Scripture. We are so used to analyzing Bible passages purely technically and forming points in our minds, that we stop allowing the text to have its way in us. The great puritan preacher John Owen famously said, 'If the Word does not dwell with power *in us*, it will not pass with power *from* us'.[14]

I find it helpful to make sure my own devotional readings are from a different text to the series I am preaching. At the moment I am preaching through Hebrews on a Sunday, but my devotional times are from Zechariah. I have deliberately chosen a very different genre for my personal Bible readings so that I can let the Scriptures speak to me, first and foremost, before thinking of how I can speak to others.

And then when I am preparing my preaching passage from Hebrews, I begin by asking God to allow the passage to speak to me. It is very possible to preach to others a passage that has not impacted your own life and your preaching will lack power and conviction as a result. A Spirit-filled preacher is one who has clothed himself in the text, allowed God's Word to make him feel uncomfortable, challenged, moved and excited, and then, and only then, is he ready to speak powerfully to others from the experience he has had with God. Be as vulnerable to the Spirit as you can be when you are preparing to preach.

Prayer life

Often we are so busy telling others about the importance of prayer, we forget how essential it is to preaching. A godly seminary professor said his ambition was to spend the same amount of time in prayer as he did in sermon preparation and he used to spend 15 hours preparing his sermons!

Often our lives are too cluttered as preachers to soak ourselves in prayer and 'drink' of the Spirit. But are we spending our time wisely? Surely we would see a lot more power in our pulpits if we devoted time to prayer. And not just 'going through the motions' prayer. But prayer that wrestles with God, like Jacob wrestling with the Angel of the Lord — transferring 'I will not let you go until you bless me' (Gen. 32: 26) into 'I will not get off my knees until you fill me with your Spirit, Lord'.

---

14 John Owen, *The Works of John Owen*, XVI, Banner of Truth, 1968, p.76.

E. M. Bounds spoke about the word 'unction', a word that is often used to describe the mysterious power of Spirit-filled preaching. He said:

> This unction comes to the preacher not in the study but in the closet. It is heaven's distillation in answer to prayer… [U]nction is not the gift of genius …It is not found in the halls of learning. No eloquence can woo it. No industry can win it. No prelatical hands can confer it. … It is heaven's distillation in answer to prayer.[15]

When was the last time you wrestled with God in prayer, admitting to him you can do nothing without him; asking for a deep cleansing from your own sin and apathy of heart; acknowledging that all spiritual authority and power in the pulpit is sent from heaven to preachers who long for it enough? How much do you want people to be spiritually transformed, rather than simply wanting approval for your sermon? How much do you want them to love God with all their beings? To what extent do you love God with all your heart and soul and mind and strength? And love his Son who spilt his blood to save you and call you to preach in power to spiritually blind men and women?

What is your deepest longing? Is it for God to be glorified? If it is, do you crave that more than a drug addict craves his heroin? If you do, then you will soak yourself in Scripture, soak yourself in prayer and rivers of living water will flow from your mouth. 'Be being filled with the Spirit.' That is the gateway to power in the pulpit. Don't settle for anything less.

---

15 E. M. Bounds, *Power through Prayer,* chapter 15. Electronic text: http://www.ntslibrary.com/PDF%20Books/Power%20Through%20Prayer%20by%20EM%20Bounds.pdf

CHAPTER 14

A call to speak:
The challenge to peach the Word

Jeremy McQuoid

W e should never under estimate the power of a public speaker. My 10 year-old son has been studying the Second World War at school and he had to prepare a talk on the life and times of Sir Winston Churchill, including many of his iconic quotes. Every year when the UK commemorates its war heroes, the words of Churchill are read out publicly,

> … we shall defend our island, whatever the cost may be.
> We shall fight on the beaches, we shall fight on the landing
> grounds, we shall fight in the fields and in the streets, we shall
> fight in the hills; we shall never surrender[16].

Many historians feel that, combined with the military strategy of Britain and her allies, it was the rhetoric of Churchill that inspired the war effort during the toughest days of WW2. He captured the mood of a nation and inspired the defiance of an army, without ever picking up a gun or a firing a canon! And seventy years later his words are part of British folklore.

And today, despite all our advances in media and technology, nothing quite compares to a preacher, in all his vulnerability, standing in front of a crowd,

---

16 Winston Churchill, f rom a speech delivered to the House of Commons, Westminster, 4th June, 1940

inspiring them, persuading them, correcting them and challenging them with his words. It will always be this way.

The Biblical Preacher

That is why the God who spoke creation into being is still calling men and women to declare his truth today through the fragile, yet gripping artistry of preaching. Charles Spurgeon said famously, 'If God calls you to preach the Gospel, don't stoop to become a king.'[17]

Spurgeon believed that biblical preaching was the most important task in the world, and this conviction grows deep in the spirit of everyone who is truly called to preach. 'How could I do anything else?'

A preacher stands between heaven and hell, holds out the hand of God to his creatures and says, 'Come and let me rescue you.' That's how dramatically Paul put it when he was talking to the Corinthians:

> We are therefore Christ's ambassadors, as though God were making his appeal through us. We implore you on Christ's behalf: be reconciled to God.
> (2 Cor.5: 20 NIV)

If you were sitting in the Oval Office of the American President, about to be appointed the next ambassador of the US to some foreign country, your heart would beat faster as the sheer weight of representing the most powerful country in the world began to dawn on you. But that is only the United States, and only a human president. The reality behind biblical preaching is that we become a mouthpiece for the God who flung stars into space and gave Saturn its rings, who breathed this vast universe into life and will roll it up one day like a scroll, who poured out his blood to redeem his image-bearing creatures from futile living.

We stand between heaven and hell, angels and demons. We are at the cutting edge of spiritual warfare, wrestling with the souls of men and women. And for some unfathomable reason, God has entrusted his gospel, the message

---

17 As quoted in Francis R Shivers, *Christian Basics 101*, Xulon Press, 2009, p.38

of his glorious Son's redeeming work for the cosmos, into our frail hands. What a calling! It may fill us with fear but we won't be lacking in motivation.

'Woe to me if I do not preach the Gospel'!

That is why a preacher called by God feels compelled to give his life for this awesome purpose. Paul said, 'woe to me if I do not preach the Gospel.'(1 Cor.9:16 NIV) Jeremiah had a very uncomfortable relationship with preaching not least because he was called to deliver messages of judgment to decadent Jerusalem. He felt the pain in his heart of delivering God's oracles of doom to the people of Jerusalem whom he loved. But he could not turn away. Once he had received the word of God, he could not hold back from declaring it in all its power:

> But if I say, "I will not mention his word
> or speak anymore in his name,"
> his word is in my heart like a fire,
> a fire shut up in my bones.
> I am weary of holding it in;
> indeed, I cannot. (Jer.20: 9)

That's what it feels like to be a preacher called of God. There is this inner compulsion to declare the oracles of God to dying men and women. Do you feel that call in your bones? Countless times I have spent hours soaking myself in a text of Scripture, feeling the weight of it coursing through my soul (the Bible never seems to deal with small issues — almost always life and death, glory and shame). And I feel this same tension Jeremiah spoke about. These things are too big for me to carry but I can't hold in what the Lord has revealed to me through his Word.

It's too big, too momentous to hide away. It's not simply that I have an opportunity to declare it. I *must declare* it like fire in my bones. That is the call to preach. To believe, at that sacred moment when a frail man opens the eternal word of God to dying people, that is the most important thing happening in the world at that moment.

It is true, as the apostle James tells us, that 'Not many of you should become teachers' (Jas. 3: 1). It is such a vital and exacting calling. But when you know you have received the call, every other duty seems to fade into the background and communicating God's Word to God's people becomes your reason for living.

'This one thing I do'

My wife reminds me about a particular Saturday evening when I was finishing my sermon (later than hoped, I confess) and she came in to say 'goodnight.' She whispered the words 'I love you' but I was so engrossed in sermon preparation that I replied, 'Amen'!

Now I am not suggesting we discard our wives for the sake of the Bible! Pastors who have done that inevitably live to regret it. But I am trying to highlight the centrality of biblical preaching not only to the health of a church and the salvation of men and woman, but for the glory of God and his ultimate victory in the cosmic conflict we join when we open his Word to his fallen image-bearers.

As a pastor in a local church, I have several responsibilities in my job. There are leadership matters to attend to regularly, people with problems in the church who I meet up to pray with and bring some direction to. And of course doing my fair share of administration. Nonetheless preaching is my main focus and has to be my main focus for the sake of the church. I need to focus on what no-one else has been called to do, and leave other jobs that perhaps several others could do with them. Preaching needs to consume you if you are to be an effective preacher.

Once, immediately after preaching, Martin Lloyd Jones was asked by the chairman of the service, how he felt. Lloyd Jones who was sweating, slumped into his chair, exhausted, and said, 'It felt like giving birth!' If you are a regular preacher, you will know exactly what Lloyd Jones meant. To preach, you battle with a text, you battle with your own heart, you wrestle with God in prayer for his power and anointing and you stand vulnerable and emotional in front of a wide range of people every week — some who are antagonistic, some who could not care less, and some whose lives are hanging on every word that comes out of your mouth.

Alistair Begg, one of the best expositors of our day, came to preach at a pastors' conference we hosted in our church. I asked him afterwards what the first thought was that went through his head after he had preached. A man who seems so sure of himself in the pulpit and so at ease with public speaking, surprised me when he said, 'I want to go straight to the car park, get in my car and drive home without speaking to anyone'.

It's not that Alistair Begg is unfriendly. It's that good preaching is so all-consuming — you feel your own vulnerability, you pour your soul out in front of people, and you do it week after week — that it leaves you physically and emotionally drained. If preaching does not consume you, you have no business preaching.

Preach the Word

That may not sound a positive invitation with which to close a preaching book. I love preaching. I would sooner have my arm chopped off than to be told I could never preach again. But if preaching is going to be all that God intends it to be, if we're to recover our confidence in Scripture and see God-glorifying preaching that transforms peoples' lives, it will take men and women of passion who have conviction that God's Word is reliable, relevant and revolutionary. Set apart men and women who are desperate to declare that word accurately, boldly and prophetically to a world full of people seeking spiritual reality.

There can be no half measures. Half-hearted preaching from biblically illiterate verbal entertainers won't do it. The nineteenth century atheist David Hume shocked his friends one day when he said he was going to hear the preaching of a local minister called John Brown. His friends asked him why he was going. Hume replied, 'it is a real luxury to me to listen to a man who believes what he preaches.' It's that kind of conviction that is going to turn the tide of Biblical preaching today. Are you ready to preach the Word? There is no greater calling in the world, no more urgent need in the church but if you are going to do it, you must do it with all your heart!

APPENDIX A

Exercises

Stephen McQuoid

Practising your introductions

Imaging you are preaching on the following passages. Try to think of the best way of introducing the subject.

John 3:1-16	Jesus' conversation with Nicodemus
Genesis 39:1-20	The temptation of Joseph
Isaiah 40:28-31	Gaining strength from God
Ephesians 6:10-20	The Armour of God
Daniel 1:1-21	Daniel in Captivity
Exodus 20:1-16	The Ten Commandments
Hosea 11:1-11	The Love of God
Hebrews 11:1-12	Faith

Practising your illustrations

Imagine you are dealing with the following verses in a sermon. Think of the best way of illustrating them.

Philippians 2: 3	Do nothing out of selfish ambition
Ephesians 4: 2	Be completely humble
Matthew 7: 16	By their fruits you will recognize them

Psalm 27: 1	The Lord is my light
Philippians 2: 6	Who, being in very nature God, did not consider equality with God something tobe grasped.
Proverbs 29: 1	A man who remains stiff-necked after many rebukes will suddenly be destroyed without remedy.
Genesis 40: 23	The chief cupbearer, however, forgot Joseph.
Revelation 2:2	I know your deeds, your hard work, and your perseverance.

APPENDIX B

Self-Assessment Form

Stephen McQuoid

Use this form to assess your preaching. Mark yourself as honestly as possible and ask a friend to do the same so that you have an objective perspective. If possible, talk about it together. Assume 10 is excellent and 1 is poor.

Introduction:

_____ Did the introduction get the audience's attention?

_____ Was the introduction relevant to the sermon?

_____ Was the introduction of reasonable length?

Subject:

_____ Was the exposition of the passage clear and accurate?

_____ Was the level or exposition relevant to the audience?

Outline:

_____ Was there a logical sequence of thought?

_____ Were the key points clearly expressed and obvious?

_____ Was there a smooth transition between points?

Illustrations:

____ Were points illustrated sufficiently and appropriately?

____ Were illustrations concise and to the point?

Application:

____ Was the application appropriate?

____ Was there sufficient application?

____ Did the message challenge the audience?

____ Was the required response from the audience made clear?

Conclusion:

____ Was the sermon summarised well?

____ Was the conclusion a suitable length?

____ Was the sermon brought to a smooth conclusion?

Voice:

____ Was the voice sufficiently loud?

____ Was there good variation in tone?

Enthusiasm:

____ Was the presentation enthusiastic?

____ Was there good eye contact?

____ Did the speaker engage well with the audience?

____ Did the speaker communicate naturally?

Observations and Comments:

APPENDIX C

A basic expository library

Stephen McQuoid

Commentaries come in different forms and should be used in different ways. There are the more basic commentaries that give you an idea about the passage as a whole (B). These are the first commentaries you are likely to read when you prepare a sermon. There are also more technical commentaries, and these would be used to look into some particularly complex aspect of a verse (T). They can be equally valuable and provide a more substantial reference guide. For this basic expository library, I will provide one recommendation of each type of commentary for the 'magisterial' books of the Bible. These recommendations are based on my personal usage of these commentaries and give an example of the kind of things to look out for.

- **Genesis**

  B Derek Kidner, *Genesis*, Tyndale Old Testament Commentary, IVP, 1967

  T Gordon Wenham, *Genesis* (2 vols) Word Biblical Commentary, Word, 1994

- **Exodus**

  B Alan Cole, *Exodus*, Tyndale Old Testament Commentary, IVP, 1973

  T John Durham, *Exodus*, Word Biblical Commentary, Word, 1987

- **Numbers**

  B Gordon J Wenham *Numbers* Tyndale Old Testament Commentary, IVP, 1981

  T Philip J Budd *Numbers,* Word Biblical Commentary, Word, 1984

- **Deuteronomy**

  B Raymond Brown, *Deuteronomy*, Bible Speaks Today, IVP, 1993

  T Gordon McConville, *Deuteronomy*, Apollos, IVP, 2002

- **1 and 2 Samuel**

  B Robert Gordon, *1&2 Samuel*, Paternoster Press, 1986

  T *1 Samuel*, Ralph Klein, Word Biblical Commentary, Word 1983
     2 Samuel, Arnold Anderson, Word Biblical Commentary, Word, 1989

- **Psalms**

  B Michael Wilcock, *Psalms* (2vols), Bible Speaks Today, IVP, 2001

  T Peter Cragie, Marvin Tate, Leslie Allen, Psalme (3 vols.), Word Biblical Commentary, Word, 1990

- **Isaiah**

  B Barry Webb, *Isaiah*, Bible Speaks Today, IVP, 1996

  T Alec Motyer, *The Prophecy of Isaiah*, IVP, 1993

- **Matthew**

  B R.T France, *Matthew*, Tyndale New Testament Commentary, IVP, 1985

  T Donald Hagner, *Matthew* (2 vols), Word Biblical Commentary, Word, 1993

- **Mark**

  B Dick France, *Mark*, Bible Reading Fellowship, 1996

  T RT France, *The Gospel of Mark*, NIGTC, Eerdmans, 2002

- **Luke**

  B David Gooding, *According to Luke*, IVP, 1987

  T Darrel Bock, *Luke* (2 vols), Baker, 1999

- **John**
  B   Leon Morris, *Reflections on John* (4vols), Baker, 1986
  T   D.A Carson, *The Gospel According to John*, IVP, 1991

- **Acts**
  B   John Stott, *The Message of Acts*, Bible Speaks Today, IVP, 1990
  T   Craig Keener, *Acts: an exegetical commentary* (4vols), Baker, 2012

- **Romans**
  B   John Stott, *The Message of Romans*, Bible Speaks Today, IVP, 1994
  T   Douglas Moo, *The Epistle to the Romans*, NICNT, Eerdmans, 1996

- **1 Corinthians**
  B   Tom Wright, *Paul for Everyone: 1 Corinthians*
  T   Anthony Thiselton, *The First Epistle to the Corinthians*, NIGTC, Eerdmans, 2000

- **Ephesians**
  B   John Stott, *The Message of Ephesians*, Bible Speaks Today, IVP, 1979
  T   Peter O'Brien, *The Letter to the Ephesians*, Apollos, 1999

- **Hebrews**
  B   Raymond Brown, *The Message of Hebrews*, Bible Speaks Today, IVP, 1982
  T   Peter O'Brien, *The Letter to the Hebrews*, Apollos, 2010

- **Revelation**
  B   William Barclay, *The Revelation of John*, St.Andrews Press, 1990
  T   G.K. Beale, *The Book of Revelation*, NIGTC, Eerdmans, 1999